Healthy Eating
for Lower Cholesterol

Daniel Green   Catherine Collins RD

Healthy Eating for Lower Cholesterol

photography by Lis Parsons

Kyle Books

To my daughter, Eleanor (Daniel Green)

For Allan, Sophie, Alex, and the Blackmores (Catherine Collins)

Introduction

Few of us ever pause to consider our heart and circulation, despite the crucial part that they play in enabling us to lead a full and active life. Often, it is only when we're running for a train or exercising at the gym that we become aware of just how hard our circulation is working to keep up with the extra demands imposed on it.

Statistics show that cardiovascular disease ("cardio"—heart; "vascular"—blood vessel) remains one of the biggest killers, claiming the life of one in five men, and one in six women; and nearly half of all deaths from coronary heart disease are due to high blood cholesterol levels. Background damage to blood vessels has already begun by the time we approach our late twenties (even though it may be another fifteen years or so before symptoms declare themselves), but by taking steps to change our diet and lifestyle we can greatly influence the health of our heart and circulation.

Time for a change

The fact that you've picked up this book indicates that you may be interested in—or perhaps concerned about—your heart health, and the risk of circulatory disease. Perhaps a health check has shown a raised cholesterol level? Or you have had a wake-up call from seeing a friend or relative suffer a stroke or heart attack and the way in which it has affected their quality of life. Or you may simply have decided that it's time to address what goes on inside your body in order to maintain your current good health well into old age.

Whatever the reason for your interest, the information in *Healthy Eating for Lower Cholesterol* will help you to choose a healthier way of eating, and you will be amazed at the abundance of foods allowed. It's a very positive diet, that, together with Dan's recipes, will give you all the inspiration you need.

The cholesterol conundrum

Of all the substances that our body produces, cholesterol seems to hold the record for bad press. Yet, what people often tend to overlook is that cholesterol is essential for human life—so important, in fact, that the body makes its own supply so that it does not have to rely on dietary intake.

What exactly is cholesterol?

Cholesterol forms the basis of steroid hormones such as testosterone and progesterone (sex hormones), cortisol (for stress adaptation), and vitamin D (for healthy bones). It also helps to build and maintain healthy cell membranes, and the insulating sheath around nerve fibers that act like "broadband," speeding nerve signals to and from the brain. Also, the liver uses cholesterol to make bile salts that help to digest food more effectively.

The majority of the cholesterol in our circulation is made by the body, mostly in the liver from saturated fat in the diet. The remainder comes from dietary sources—animal foods such as fatty meat, eggs, dairy foods, seafood, fish, and poultry. The liver controls blood cholesterol levels, reducing the body's natural cholesterol production when cholesterol from the diet is available.

The Cholesterol Couriers

Cholesterol has to travel from the liver to wherever it is needed in the body, so transport via the circulation is inevitable. Cholesterol is too "waxy" to dissolve in blood, so it is transported around the body in a number of tiny "couriers," called lipoproteins. A blood cholesterol level reflects the amount of cholesterol transported by these lipoprotein couriers at the time of a blood test. In general, a high blood cholesterol level increases your risk of cardiovascular disease. However, some couriers are considered "safer" than others, so the goal of cholesterol management is to lower the levels of unsafe couriers, while maintaining more stable forms of cholesterol transport.

Just as vehicles on the road vary in size, so do our cholesterol couriers. Unlike road traffic, however, each lipoprotein can be remodeled by the liver into another type, changing its composition in the process. So, while they may start out as very large, buoyant, and rich in fat, they gradually shrink in size, becoming smaller, denser cholesterol couriers, carrying less fat.

LDL ("bad" cholesterol)

Low-density lipoprotein (LDL) is the main cholesterol courier in our circulation; it transports cholesterol and triglycerides (fats) from cells that produce more than they can use to cells and tissues in need. Around 70 percent of our circulating cholesterol is carried by LDL couriers. They vary in size depending on their triglyceride and cholesterol content —in healthy individuals LDL carriers are large and relatively few in number; in contrast small, dense LDL carriers are strongly associated with heart and circulatory disease, possibly because their small size allows them to penetrate the artery walls. LDL cholesterol is often termed "bad" cholesterol for this reason, but its level can be reduced by diet and lifestyle changes.

Other cholesterol couriers

In addition to LDL, there are other transport couriers for cholesterol. Chylomicron couriers transport cholesterol and dietary fat from the digestive tract to the liver, and very low-density lipoproteins (VLDLs) then haul triglycerides around the body for uptake by cells requiring fat, before returning to the liver for reprocessing into LDL couriers. VLDL couriers may be likened to manufacturers' lorries, delivering large quantities of goods (triglycerides) to a central warehouse for collection by the LDL couriers. Triglycerides are an independent risk factor for cardiovascular disease, often raised in people who are overweight, drink too much alcohol, or have Type 2 diabetes (see page 19). Controlling blood sugar, and reducing alcohol intake controls blood triglycerides.

HDL ("good" cholesterol)

The smallest lipoprotein, high-density lipoprotein (HDL), is made in the liver from the remains of LDL cholesterol. Unlike other cholesterol couriers, HDL offers a "collection" rather than "delivery" service, collecting surplus cholesterol and fat from cells, and returning them to the liver for processing and removal. HDL also has the ability to "pull" cholesterol and fat from newly formed deposits on the artery walls, helping to maintain healthy arteries.

Once excess cholesterol has been returned to the liver, it can be converted into bile acids for transfer to the gallbladder, or it can be recycled into lipoprotein couriers again. Each day the liver produces up to 2g of cholesterol and 0.4g of bile salts, the latter to replenish losses from the bile salt pool. Reducing the recycling of bile salts is how cholesterol-lowering stanol and sterol esters (see page 34) and soluble fiber function (see page 24).

How can I check my cholesterol levels?

The only way to establish your exact cholesterol profile is by having a blood test—often called a lipid profile. Lipid is a collective term for fats in the blood, and a blood test can tell you how much cholesterol is present, and what type. A random blood test can measure total and HDL cholesterol levels. A fasting blood test (where you fast for at least 12 hours beforehand, drinking nothing but water) can measure LDL cholesterol and triglyceride levels in addition, giving a more comprehensive result.

Ideal cholesterol levels

The goal of cholesterol management is to reduce the risk of cardiovascular disease. To put this into some sort of context, a high cholesterol level alone is thought to be responsible for 46 percent of all premature deaths from coronary heart disease in the UK. Population studies may suggest a ballpark value for cholesterol levels, but our own individual cholesterol level and risk of cardiovascular disease are tempered by our lifestyle and other health concerns, such as high blood pressure. The table below gives guideline levels for each of the cholesterol couriers for general health, but the more stringent goals (the "optimal" levels) have been devised by the six leading societies dealing with cardiovascular disease in the UK. Both sets of values are relevant for the general population. If you also have diabetes, high blood pressure, or rheumatoid arthritis, then the optimal rather than guideline values should be your goal.

How is cholesterol measured?

Cholesterol is measured in "mmols," a measurement of cholesterol concentration in each litre of blood (mmol/L). This is a world standard unit for measuring cholesterol except in the USA, where the preferred measurement is the weight of cholesterol in each 100ml of blood (mg/dL). Ideal blood cholesterol levels are quoted in both measurements (see table).

A simple way to remember the desirable level of cholesterol couriers is that <u>H</u>DL should be High, <u>L</u>DL should be Low, and <u>V</u>LDL (akin to triglyceride level) should be Very Low!

Guideline cholesterol levels
Total cholesterol: 195mg/dL
   (5 mmol/L), or less
LDL cholesterol: 115mg/dL (3 mmol/L),
   or less
Triglycerides: 57mg/dL (1.5 mmol/L),
   or less
HDL cholesterol: 35mg/dL
   (0.9 mmol/L)

Optimal levels
Total cholesterol: 156mg/dL
   (4 mmol/L), or less
LDL cholesterol: 77mg/dL (2 mmol/L),
   or less
HDL cholesterol: above 58mg/dL
   (1.5 mmol/L)

The Artery Highways

In order for the couriers to be able to deliver their loads effectively and safely, they need a healthy system to travel by— that is the arteries, veins, and capillaries. Research suggests that we should not consider our total and LDL cholesterol levels in isolation, but also how well our arteries are maintained. The health of our artery highways and their ability to resist damage are the focus of most new research into cardiovascular disease.

Our body works hard to keep our artery surfaces fully repaired and so less prone to damage. Arteries are made of three layers. A strong outer "coat" surrounds a middle layer of muscles that allow the artery to widen or contract as needed to control our blood pressure. An inner layer of smooth, flat cells (called the "endothelium") creates the "non-stick" inner lining of the artery that makes for smooth blood flow. The endothelium protects the artery, repelling toxic substances and marshaling defences if the blood vessel becomes inflamed or damaged. "Resurfacing" of damaged endothelium is achieved by the components of a healthy diet (see pages 20–33).

How a cholesterol plaque is formed

In much the same way that a lorry will sometimes hit a pothole in a road, causing it to shed some of its load, naturally occurring damage to the smooth endothelium surface can encourage circulating LDL to deposit cholesterol. This then burrows below the endothelium layer, settling onto the muscular middle layer of the artery. Less stable LDL couriers (for example, those carrying "oxidized" cholesterol), are more likely to deposit their unstable cholesterol load.

At this early stage, HDL couriers traveling along the artery may notice the cholesterol deposit, and can collect it from the artery wall for return to the liver, thus preventing development of an atheroma (or plaque). If it is not collected, however, the deposit generates local inflammation *within* the artery wall, attracting the interest of passing white blood cells. These then enter the breach and successfully attack the cholesterol, but in so doing become entrapped beneath the artery surface, forming a foam-like deposit.

Finally, in a sort of damage-limitation exercise, the endothelium surface forms a protective fibrin cap, resealing the surface and entombing the cholesterol, white blood cells, and other debris (collectively known as an atheroma, or plaque) within the blood vessel wall. Remodeling of the fibrin "cap" over the plaque eventually leads to a scar resistant to the natural "stretch" of the artery wall. This hardening effect on the arteries is called atherosclerosis.

Over time, the atheroma increases in size. Initially it is accommodated by an outward bulge in the artery wall (called an "aneurysm"). Eventually, however, the strong outer coat of the artery resists any further bulge, and the atheroma begins to push inward, often rupturing the fibrin cap formed long ago to contain it. This has two possible outcomes. Either the rupture will attract red blood cells to form another clot to reseal, that can be dislodged into the circulation, eventually blocking a smaller blood vessel "downstream"; or the ruptured plaque may shower atheroma debris into the circulation, with the same devastating outcome.

These are the principal mechanisms of a catastrophic heart attack or stroke occurring without warning, often resulting in major disability or death. Using ultrasound, it has been shown, frighteningly, that unstable plaque can rupture when as little as 20 percent of a blood vessel is obstructed by an atheroma.

The effects on health of atherosclerosis

As well as cardiovascular catastrophies there are chronic symptoms associated with atherosclerosis, or hardening of the arteries, and these can compromise quality of life.

Angina is a pain across the chest, and sometimes the arms, shoulders, or jaw, brought on by exercise. The extra demands made on the heart by exercise increase its need for oxygen, but "furred" arteries have lost the ability to dilate, preventing the demands for additional blood to the heart muscle from being met. The resulting pain is the heart sustaining something similar to a "stitch in the side," and relief is experienced only when exercise is stopped and the heart has restored its oxygen demands.

Peripheral vascular disease (PVD) is the obstruction (by atherosclerosis) of the large leg arteries. Failure to meet the metabolic demands of the legs and feet during walking can cause severe pain (termed intermittent claudication), hampering mobility.

Transient ischaemic attack (TIA) is caused by a temporary disturbance of blood supply to the brain. Transient ischaemic attack is often referred to as a "mini-stroke" and is usually caused by a small blood clot blocking an artery in the brain, resulting in brief brain dysfunction and generally lasting for less than 24 hours before recovery is made. TIAs are a warning of the potential for a more devastating stroke, so are treated seriously by doctors.

The cholesterol–circulation link

Since as far back as the 1950s it has been known that raised blood cholesterol—particularly LDL cholesterol—increases your risk of heart and circulatory disease. But until recently it has been unclear as to exactly why cardiovascular disease can occur in people with normal cholesterol levels.

That each developing plaque represents a tiny pocket of inflammation within the artery wall has helped researchers to prove that any inflammation in the body—obvious or not—will affect how robust the artery will be in terms of resisting damage.

Inflammation is now considered a major cause of damage to the endothelium surface, priming an inflammatory process that accelerates the rate of cholesterol deposition and, by extension, atherosclerosis. It has been shown that people with rheumatoid arthritis—a severe inflammatory condition—have twice the risk of death from cardiovascular disease when compared with the general population. Reducing inflammation within the body is, therefore, a prime target for cholesterol control.

Reducing Your Risk Factors

Medical research has helped to determine risk factors that identify those at high risk of cardiovascular disease. There are some factors that you can't change, including advancing age or a genetic predisposition; most, however, can be modified by changes in your diet or lifestyle.

In addition to a raised blood cholesterol, the following are all major causes of premature death from cardiovascular disease:

• lack of physical activity
• smoking
• obesity
• high blood pressure

And the more risk factors you have, the higher your risk of coronary heart disease.

Physical activity

Our modern lifestyle does little to encourage regular exercise, and many of us take no physical activity during a typical week. Individuals recording less than half an hour's physical activity a week are almost three times more likely to die in the short term than those who are more active.

Regular activity has proven positive health benefits, particularly for heart health. A single exercise session can beneficially reduce triglyceride levels by an average of 20 percent, and raise HDL cholesterol by 10 percent. Regular exercise leads to favorable changes in blood pressure, blood lipids, blood glucose, insulin, and clotting factors. It also reduces the risk of circulatory disease, and slows the enlargement of any existing atheroma. What's more, the calories expended during regular exercise help with weight management, and increasing muscle tone improves blood sugar and cholesterol levels.

Fortunately, gym membership isn't required for this benefit! Thirty minutes a day of regular activity such as brisk walking, gardening, cycling, or dancing are all beneficial, but any exercise is

	FACTORS THAT INCREASE CHOLESTEROL LEVELS	FACTORS THAT INCREASE INFLAMMATION LEVELS
FACTORS YOU CAN'T CHANGE	▸ Increasing age and in particular being over 45 ▸ Being male ▸ Genetic predisposition to heart disease	▸ High blood levels of inflammatory blood proteins: homocysteine and C-reactive protein (CRP) ▸ Background inflammatory states, e.g. arthritis
FACTORS YOU CAN CHANGE	▸ Inactivity and a lack of exercise ▸ Smoking ▸ Obesity/being overweight ▸ High saturated fat intake ▸ High intake of trans fats ▸ Excess alcohol intake ▸ Uncontrolled stress and anger	▸ Smoking ▸ Obesity/being overweight ▸ High saturated fat intake ▸ High intake of trans fats ▸ High intake of plant-based polyunsaturates (omega-6) ▸ Poorly controlled diabetes ▸ High blood pressure ▸ Low or absent intake of omega-3 polyunsaturates ▸ Lack of antioxidant nutrients ▸ Excess alcohol intake ▸ Excessive iron intake

proven to be better than none. You should walk or exercise enough to leave you feeling warm and slightly out of breath. If you are unused to physical exertion, gradually build it up over several weeks.

Smoking

Smoking is a major cause of heart disease, other circulatory diseases, and cancer, and there is no "safe" level of usage. Smoking a pack of cigarettes a day doubles the risk of a heart attack.

The effects of smoking are three-fold. Nicotine constricts arteries, reducing blood supply to the heart and other tissues. Carbon monoxide from inhaled smoke reduces the amount of oxygen that can be carried in the bloodstream, and the combination of reduced oxygen delivery from reduced blood supply can damage the heart and other tissues. Nicotine and free radicals released from inhaled smoke damage the endothelium, initiating and accelerating atherosclerosis. Smoking also increases the levels of blood–clotting proteins, increases blood pressure, and lowers levels of "good" HDL cholesterol—a combination that is damaging to the heart and other tissues.

To continue smoking removes any health benefits possible from other advice in this book. Take advantage of "stop smoking" campaigns to save your health.

Obesity

Obesity is an increasing health risk in the Western world. Most adults are overweight, and obesity impacts significantly on good health. Obesity is associated with an increased risk of diabetes and hypertension (high blood pressure), that alone and together are associated with an accelerated rate of atherosclerosis.

Body fat is not inert, but generates biologically active substances (called adipokines) capable of increasing background inflammation, and accelerating atherosclerosis. Healthy people with a higher body weight have higher blood levels of protein markers of inflammation (such as C-reactive protein, or CRP), and a three-fold increased risk of heart disease—and this is the case whether or not blood cholesterol levels are raised.

Losing just 10 percent of your body weight if you are overweight carries significant health benefits, reducing the release of adipokines from the diminished body fat stores. Crash dieting is not the answer, but following a healthy diet with modest calorie restriction (between 1400 and 1800 calories a day) will result in weight loss. Every 1.1lbs (0.5kg) of fat contains the equivalent of 3500 calories, so reducing calorie intake to 500 calories a day below your body's energy needs (see box) will help you to lose 1.1lbs (0.5kg) of fat per week.

Apple or pear?

The area in which your body stores its excess fat can influence health risks. A "pear" shape (in which excess fat is stored

Average energy needs of adults (taken from COMA Report, *Dietary Reference Values*, 1991)		
AGE	MEN: CALORIES PER DAY	WOMEN: CALORIES PER DAY
19–50 years	2550	1940
50–64 years	2380	1900
65–74 years	2330	1900
75+ years	2100	1810

around the hips and thighs) carries a lower cardiovascular risk than an "apple" shape (in which body fat is stored around the waist). "Apples" have higher levels of background inflammation, easily measured using blood protein markers. They also are more likely to have insulin resistance (increasing the likelihood of diabetes), in tandem with a high blood pressure, cholesterol, and triglycerides. A combination of obesity, insulin resistance, and other factors is referred to as the "metabolic syndrome."

Waist measurements rather than weight alone more accurately identify whether people are at risk of heart disease. Test yourself by comparing your waist size with the guide on the following page, and measuring your waist midway distant from the lower rib and the hip bone. Your tape measure should cross the belly button, not swing low "below the bulge" as your trouser waistband might.

Waist measurements			
	IDEAL VALUE	INCREASED RISK—SHOULD NOT INCREASE WEIGHT FURTHER	SUBSTANTIAL RISK—SHOULD ACTIVELY TRY TO LOSE WEIGHT
Women	32in or less	32in or more	35in or more
Men	38in or less	38in or more	41in or more

Waist-to-hip ratio (WHR)

This ratio appears to be a more beneficial guide in identifying people at risk of cardiovascular disease across all weight ranges. Measure the widest part of your hips, then divide your waist measurement by your hip measurement. For example, if your waist is 32 inches, and your hip size is 38½ inches, your WHR = $32 \div 38\frac{1}{2}$ = 0.83. An ideal value is 0.83 for women, and 0.90 for men. Any waist-to-hip ratio above these values is a strong predictor for cardiovascular disease.

Clothing sizes

Recent research in nutrition has shown that, in the absence of weighing scales or a tape measure, clothing sizes can be a useful marker for risk of cardiovascular disease. For men, a trouser waist size greater than 38 inches in US/UK sizing, or 97cm in European sizing, predicts a greatly increased risk of heart disease, high blood pressure and diabetes. For women, a size 16 or above (size 18 in the UK or 48 in Europe) carries similar health risks.

Diet

The main influence on cholesterol levels from our diet is the amount and type of fat that we consume (see pages 26–32), but other factors also play a part. A regular, modest alcohol intake appears to have some cardioprotective benefits, helping your liver to form more of the beneficial HDL cholesterol. A high alcohol intake, however, will remove any such benefits because of its toxic effects on the liver. (See also page 32.)

Following the dietary advice in the next section will naturally increase your intake of dietary antioxidant nutrients to help protect your body against free-radical damage.

Stress

In moderation, mental and physical stress appear to be beneficial to the body. However, sustained high levels of stress injures blood vessels, promotes atherosclerosis, and increases circulating levels of the blood-clotting protein fibrinogen, more than doubling your risk

of cardiovascular disease. The stress hormones cortisol and adrenalin are behind these changes. A person with an angry, hostile personality has a significantly increased risk of cardiovascular disease.

Diabetes

Diabetes is on the increase in the Western world, and it is estimated that for every person diagnosed with the condition, another remains undiagnosed.

Type I diabetes occurs when the body switches off insulin production. This type requires lifelong control of blood sugar levels by injection of insulin. The most common type of diabetes is Type 2 diabetes, caused not by a lack of insulin, but by insulin resistance. In Type 2 diabetes, the body produces insulin, but its effect in clearing excessive blood sugar levels is compromised by "resistance" of body cells to accept it. Type 2 diabetes is linked to obesity, particularly central obesity with extra weight around the waist. Losing weight improves insulin usage and blood sugar levels, and also reduces the increased risk of cardiovascular disease.

High blood pressure

Blood pressure is the force of blood pushing against the artery walls, and it is necessary to ensure that blood supply can reach every cell in the body. A blood pressure reading comprises two numbers, one appearing above the other: e.g., 120/80 (an ideal reading). The higher figure (120 in this case) is the systolic pressure, representing the surge in pressure generated with every heartbeat. The lower figure (80) represents the diastolic pressure—the background pressure of blood between heartbeats.

Blood pressure varies throughout the day, being lowest when you sleep and rising when you get up, or when you are exercising, nervous, or stressed. Transient rises in blood pressure are the body's way of adapting to its environment and are perfectly normal. However, if your blood pressure constantly measures 140/90 or higher, you have high blood pressure (also called hypertension). Left unmanaged, hypertension can cause the heart to enlarge as it needs to work harder. It can also accelerate damage to the arteries, facilitating the process of atherosclerosis (see page 14) and increasing the risk of cardiovascular disease and kidney damage.

High blood pressure should not be ignored, and can be controlled with a healthy diet, adopting the Mediterranean style of eating (see page 20) in tandem with reduced salt and alcohol intake. If you are overweight, losing 10 percent of your body weight will help to lower blood pressure. Increasing physical activity levels and, if necessary, medication can also help to control the condition.

In a nutshell

So, to summarize, maintaining a healthy heart and circulation requires a two-pronged approach: control of cholesterol has a significant effect on health and, at the same time, addressing health, diet, and lifestyle issues can help to reduce inflammation within the body, protecting the artery walls from damage.

Blood pressure readings

CLASSIFICATION	SYSTOLIC BLOOD PRESSURE (mmHg)*	DIASTOLIC BLOOD PRESSURE (mmHg)
Ideal	Less than 120	Less than 80
Normal	Less than 130	Less than 85
High normal (pre-hypertensive)	131–139	85–89
Hypertension	140 or above	90 or above

*mmHg = millimeters of mercury.

The Heart-healthy Diet

In the 1960s an ambitious medical trial was devised to compare diet, lifestyle, and ongoing heart disease rates across seven countries, selected at the time for their recognized differences in heart disease rates. Led by Dr Ancel Keys, an eminent American physiologist, the results proved revolutionary, demonstrating a five- to tenfold difference in the rates of heart disease between populations.

The "Seven Countries Study," as it became known, provided evidence that a diet abundant in vegetables, fruit, pasta, bread, and olive oil, and sparing with meat, eggs, butter, and full-fat dairy products, reduced the occurrence of heart disease. It also highlighted that it was the type rather than the amount of dietary fat that had an effect. A higher intake of olive oil and omega-3 polyunsaturates from oily fish appeared to reduce the risk of heart disease and cancer. The population of Crete had the lowest rate of death from heart disease, and the longest life expectancy of all the countries studied, hence this healthful diet became known simply as the "Mediterranean diet."

Of course, there is not just one Mediterranean diet, since the countries surrounding the Mediterranean—from Africa to Europe—incorporate many cultural and food differences. Yet despite this, there are also many similarities, including an emphasis on plant-based foods (vegetables, fruit, legumes, and wholegrains), along with a relatively low consumption of meat, a moderate intake of low-fat dairy products, modest alcohol intake, and a relatively high intake of olive oil.

Key aspects of the cardioprotective Mediterranean diet

▸ Abundance of vegetables, salads, and fruit, rich in cardioprotective nutrients
▸ High in monounsaturated fats, such as extra virgin olive oil
▸ Balanced omega-3/omega-6 polyunsaturated fat ratio
▸ Emphasis on wholegrain breads and cereals, and legumes
▸ Moderate amounts of lean meat, fish, dairy foods, and eggs
▸ Only a small amount of alcohol

There are two key nutritional approaches to reducing cardiovascular disease and maintaining good health. First, controlling the level and type of circulating cholesterol will minimize the risk of LDL cholesterol offloading into the artery wall. Second, reducing background inflammation in the body reduces the sensitivity of the endothelium, improving its ability to defend the artery against attack from blood cholesterol, blood sugar, or high blood pressure.

The Mediterranean diet deftly addresses both of these concerns, as well as aiding in the prevention and improved management of other chronic diseases such as high blood pressure, diabetes, and cancer.

Being a whole diet, as opposed to so many others that concentrate on a specific factor, such as fat intake, for example, the Mediterranean diet has the edge for a number of reasons:

▸ The wide variety of foods makes it easy to follow—for lifelong benefit
▸ The high antioxidant content of the diet (being abundant in vegetables, fruit, and extra virgin olive oil) reduces heart disease and cancer risk, and can improve the symptoms and management of other chronic diseases
▸ It is a style of eating that can be adapted to different populations, tailored to local foods, but always maintaining the same health benefits. Many Asian countries, for example, have diets with a similar profile (sometimes termed MediterrAsian!) and also enjoy low rates of cardiovascular disease.

The next section expands on what makes a diet "Mediterranean," and explains how certain foods can complement each other to enhance the health benefits. The closer you can make your diet to the Mediterranean model, the better your cholesterol control will be and, with it, the likelihood of healthy arteries.

Fruit and vegetables in the cardioprotective diet

"Eat more fruit and vegetables" is the simple yet profound health message that forms the cornerstone of the Mediterranean diet. A high vegetable and

fruit intake is common in healthy populations enjoying a low incidence of heart disease, stroke and cancer. Vegetables and fruit are nature's own "functional foods," so powerful that the World Health Organisation recommends a daily intake of at least 14 ounces (400g) a day—loosely translated as the "five a day" with which most of us are now familiar. Fresh, frozen, canned, and dried fruits and vegetables and their juices all "count" toward the daily five. Despite this, however, few of us manage even a scant three portions a day.

Nature's functional foods

Fruit and vegetables provide us with a host of plant substances that are essential for health. Phytochemicals (see right) and dietary fibers enhance their natural "functionality" and their low calorie content offsets the calorie-rich Western diet that contributes to obesity. The average Mediterranean diet provides around 125 calories per 3½ ounces (100g) of food eaten, compared with 160 calories per 3½ ounces (100g) in the typical Western diet. Adopting this way of eating is a sure way to eat a lot more and weigh a lot less.

The antioxidants present in fruit and vegetables include vitamins, minerals, and phytochemicals (plant chemicals). Vitamin C, beta carotene, vitamin E, zinc, and selenium protect the body from damaging "free radicals," natural by-products of oxygen metabolism within cells. Free radicals can be harnessed for useful purposes but a surplus can cause cell and tissue injury. Certain lifestyle aspects, such as smoking and excessive sun exposure, are also known to trigger excessive free-radical production.

Vitamins and minerals

Fruit and vegetables provide an abundance of vitamins and minerals— tiny nutrients essential for life and that support and protect the body in a myriad of ways. The B group vitamins, for example, help to release energy in the cells, protect against anaemia, and to maintain a healthy skin and nerve supply. Folic acid—a B vitamin found naturally in green leafy vegetables, oranges, and pulses—works with vitamins B6 and B12 to reduce blood levels of homocysteine (a toxic by-product of protein metabolism known to cause damage to the endothelium and increase the risk of heart disease and stroke).

Phytochemicals

Plants contain hundreds of non-nutrient substances called "phytochemicals" that provide the wide range of colors and flavors present in fruit and vegetables. As each color supplies a different class of phytochemical, it is important to ensure

What counts as a five-a-day portion?

The servings below should give you an idea of what comprises a "portion":
1 apple, pear, or banana
1 handful of grapes, strawberries, or cherries
2 tomatoes, plums, or satsumas
1 large slice of melon
²/₃ cup fruit juice
1 tablespoon dried fruit/3 dried apricots
1 dessert bowl mixed salad
2 tablespoons cooked vegetables

Notes: Potatoes do not "count" as a portion and each item can "count" only once, irrespective of the amount eaten—it is the blend of colors and flavors that gives synergism to the plant-chemical benefits (so eating two or more apples, for example, is therefore just more of the same). (See also Phytochemicals above.)

that your diet includes an assortment of colors in order to enhance the usefulness of the fruit and vegetables you are eating.

The importance of phytochemicals in providing additional health benefits beyond those of vitamin and mineral intake is increasingly recognized. Many possess powerful antioxidant abilities that are far greater than the effects of established antioxidant nutrients such as vitamin C. For example, lutein helps to protect the eye retina from UV light damage and lycopene protects against prostate cancer. Beta-carotene (derived from foods, not from high-dose supplements) seems to have protective properties against cancer, in tandem with vitamin C and E intake.

Flavonoids such as quercetin enhance vitamin C function, and catechins (found in tea) provide a substantial antioxidant load. Cocoa flavonoids have cardiovascular benefit, reducing LDL cholesterol, blood stickiness, and background inflammation. So two squares of dark chocolate daily with a minimum 70 percent cocoa solid content provide a substantial flavonoid load without excessive calorie or fat intake. The range of colors in extra virgin olive oil reflects its polyphenol content, providing antioxidant benefits. The deeper the color (green or yellow), the higher the polyphenol content. Paler colored, refined olive oils lack the polyphenol content.

Where to find your phytochemicals

ANTIOXIDANT PHYTOCHEMICALS:	FOUND IN:
Lutein (carotenoid)	Corn, spinach, kale, E161b food coloring
Lycopene (carotenoid)	Tomatoes, watermelons, pink grapefruit, papayas, rosehips
Beta-carotene	Carrots, tomatoes, peppers, pumpkins
Anthocyanins	Eggplant, cherries, red grapes, blackberries, blackcurrants, bilberries, red cabbages, E163 food coloring
Quercetin	Citrus fruits, green and black tea, onions, apples, broccoli
Catechins	Tea, chocolate, apples

Fat and calorie content of nuts and seeds*

NUTS	G FAT PER 100G	CALORIES PER 100G
Chestnuts	3g	170 calories
Sunflower seeds	48g	581 calories
Groundnuts	50g	589 calories
Cashews	48g	573 calories
Pistachios	55g	601 calories
Almonds	57g	621 calories
Sesame seeds	58g	598 calories
Brazil nuts	68g	682 calories
Walnuts	69g	688 calories

*All values given are for an edible portion, not including shells.

Nuts

Frequent nut consumption appears to offer some protection against heart disease. Diets supplemented with nuts, particularly almonds and walnuts, show a beneficial reduction in LDL cholesterol and total cholesterol, and a significant reduction in coronary heart disease risk. Regular nut and seed consumption (around 5 ounces per week) reduces the levels of inflammatory proteins, indicating that nuts and seeds can help protect against

arterial damage. Nuts also provide protein, magnesium, copper, vitamin E, folic acid, fiber, potassium, and the essential fatty acid alpha-linolenic acid (particularly walnuts). Nuts are high in fats, but mainly in the heart-healthy unsaturated fats. The one exception is coconut—this is high in saturated fat, although it is a different type from the animal-based equivalent. The jury is still out as to whether or not coconut oil is a health risk.

Legumes

Pulses such as peas, beans, and lentils are excellent sources of insoluble fiber (roughage) and cholesterol-lowering soluble fiber. They are also rich in cardio-protective nutrients such as vitamin E, B vitamins, folic acid, calcium, iron, and zinc. They are naturally low in fat and are a useful source of protein that can replace or extend meat or fish dishes. Dried pulses require initial soaking followed by prolonged cooking in accordance with their label so as to remove natural toxins. Canned beans and pulses contain the same nutritional benefits.

The "gel"-type soluble fiber found in pulses and porridge oats can bind not only dietary cholesterol, but a proportion of cholesterol-containing bile salts, preventing re-uptake for recycling by the liver, and therefore beneficially depleting the body cholesterol "pool." Further along the bowel, soluble fibers can act as a natural fuel source for friendly bacteria, helping to maintain a healthy bowel.

Soybeans

Soybeans deserve a special mention for their established health benefits, particularly in relation to heart disease, cancer, osteoporosis, and women's health. Traditional soy foods include soybeans, miso, soybean milk and oil, margarine, soybean sauce, tempeh, tofu, and tofu products. Soybean protein concentrates, soybean protein isolates, and textured vegetable protein (TVP) are more modern ways of including soybean in the diet.

A daily intake of 25g (1 ounce) of soybean protein can reduce LDL cholesterol by 10 percent, sufficient to permit a UK health claim on foods that provide more than 5g of soybean protein per serving. In practice, non-vegetarians often find 25g (1 ounce) of soybean protein daily difficult to achieve. For example, one soybean yogurt provides 5g of soya protein, and 250ml (1 cup) of soybean milk provides around 10g of soybean protein. The benefits of soybean protein appear to be dose-related—lower intakes having a lesser effect on blood cholesterol.

Not everyone appears to gain from this protein. Research has shown that to receive the cholesterol-lowering benefits requires an ability to convert soybean phytochemicals (called isoflavones) into a weak estrogen called equol. It is this effect—soybean protein plus equol—that lowers LDL cholesterol. A third or more of the population lacks the facility to do this, and so do not benefit from its inclusion. It is not possible to predict whether or not you can produce equol.

However, like all beans, soybeans remain a useful source of soluble fiber, and a healthy substitute for animal protein, and so are still recommended.

Wholegrain cereals in the heart-healthy diet

People in Mediterranean countries tend to consume a wide variety of carbohydrate foods derived from wholegrain cereals, vegetables, and legumes. Bread, pasta, rice, bulghur, couscous, and potato should form part of each meal to make it filling rather than fattening.

Wholegrains such as wheat, corn, barley, oats, and rye provide important cardioprotective nutrients including the B group vitamins, antioxidant vitamins, zinc, and selenium. These nutrients, along with their beneficial levels of dietary fiber, confer the positive health benefits of whole grains.

Wholegrain carbohydrates provide the main dietary source of insoluble fiber, or roughage, adding bulk, improving bowel function, and preventing constipation. In addition, starchy foods also provide the soluble (gel-type) fiber that slows down the digestion of foods, helping to regulate appetite, improve blood glucose levels, and reduce cholesterol. Soluble fiber contributes to the viscosity of the food, slowing the rate of carbohydrate digestion and giving a sustained release of sugars that improve blood sugar control and increase HDL cholesterol.

The speed at which sugars are liberated from carbohydrate digestion, causing a rise in blood sugar level, can be gauged by the glycaemic index value of a food, also known as GI. Glycemic load (GL) is the GI value of a food adjusted for its carbohydrate content per portion. For example, watermelon has a high GI (from fruit sugar), but each slice provides such a small amount of sugar that it has virtually no influence on blood sugar levels and so it has a low GL value. Low-GI/GL foods produce a modest but sustained rise in blood sugar, considered more beneficial than the rapid peak in blood sugars provided by high-GI foods. The Mediterranean diet automatically gives you a low-GI diet. "Slow carb"—not "low carb"—is the healthy choice.

Oats

Oats are rich in beta-glucan, a gel-like fiber that helps to lower blood cholesterol level, to sustain blood sugar levels, and to maintain bowel health. The minimum effective daily dose appears to be around 3g of beta-glucan. Oat bran provides 5.5g and rolled oats 4g of beta-glucan per 100g (3½ ounce) serving. Foods providing at least 0.75g (or a quarter) of the effective 3g dose are allowed to make a health claim on marketing literature.

Note: Beta-glucan in yeast and mushrooms is slightly different and has none of the same beneficial effects.

Fats in the Mediterranean diet

Fat is vital in our diet, providing energy, fat-soluble vitamins (vitamins A, D, E, and K), and the essential fats—linoleic acid and alpha-linolenic acid—that the body cannot make. Fat is the most energy-dense nutrient in the diet, providing 9 calories per gram – that's over double the 4 calories per gram from carbohydrates or protein. This calorie load is the same whether the fat is solid at room temperature (as in butter or lard), or liquid (as in vegetable oils). Thus the calorie load of a single wrapped butter pat is the same as that of a teaspoon of any oil – around 45 calories. All fats should be limited if you are trying to lose weight.

Fat confers certain sensory properties, increasing the appeal of foods, affecting the taste, texture, appearance, and "mouthfeel" of a food and making it palatable. The combination of taste and energy load is probably the reason why nearly 40 percent of the total energy in our diet comes from fat. However, too much fat, or the wrong type, increases blood cholesterol levels and background inflammation, damaging arteries and increasing the risk of heart disease. For this reason, present guidelines recommend that around just 35 percent of our energy should come from fat, with no more than 10 percent of that being from saturated fat.

It's easy to calculate an ideal fat and saturated fat intake. Choose a daily calorie intake, and divide by 27 to get the grams of total fat, or by 91 for the maximum saturated fat intake each day (see table on facing page).

A quick guide to fats in the diet

TYPE OF FAT	PREDOMINANT SOURCES	EFFECT ON BLOOD CHOLESTEROL	EFFECT ON INFLAMMATION
Monounsaturated	Olive oil, rapeseed (canola) oil, groundnuts and groundnut oil, almonds, avocado	Lowers LDL Increases HDL	Decreases inflammation
Polyunsaturated omega-3 rich	Oily fish (dark-fleshed), algae, some eggs, flaxseed (linseed), green leafy vegetables	Lowers triglycerides Lowers LDL (EPA and DHA) ALA (see page 30) —no effect	Decreases inflammation
Polyunsaturated omega-6 rich	Corn, sunflower, soybeans and soybean oil, walnut and walnut oils, safflower oils	Lowers LDL Increases HDL slightly	Increases inflammation
Saturated	Butter, lard, cheese, fatty meat, palm oil, hydrogenated fats, ice cream	Increases LDL Increases HDL	Increases inflammation
Trans fats	Hydrogenated oils found in processed foods, pastry, biscuits	Increases LDL Lowers HDL	Increases inflammation

How are fats named?

There are three main types of fat in our food—saturated, monounsaturated, and polyunsaturated—and all dietary fats contain a mixture of the three. The names relate to their structural differences, with small variations having large health effects on cholesterol levels and inflammation. Fats are named according to the type present in the largest amount (see table above). Olive oil, for example, is classified as a monounsaturated fat even though it contains saturates and polyunsaturates, because monounsaturates make up 75 per cent of its content.

Saturated fats

Traditional diets obtained saturated fats from animal sources such as meat and dairy products, and these foods were identified by the Seven Countries Study (see page 20) as an increased cardiovascular risk. Saturated fat increases blood cholesterol levels. The higher the saturated fat intake, the higher the blood cholesterol level. Saturated fats also increase background levels of inflammation, "sensitizing" the artery wall to damage.

Foods naturally high in cholesterol (such as liver, egg yolks, shrimp, and shellfish) have little effect on blood cholesterol levels. This is because they contain little saturated fat, and the cholesterol they provide is offset by reduced cholesterol production by the liver.

Nowadays saturated fats are not confined to animal products. Processed foods often contain hydrogenated vegetable oils. Hydrogenation "hardens" the oil, increasing its saturated fat content beyond that of the parent oil. In addition, the hydrogenation process can produce "trans" fats rather than the naturally occurring "cis" form. "Cis" and "trans" are terms used to describe the shape of the fat after hydrogenation. Hydrogenated cis fats can be easily used by the body, but trans fats have a different shape that the body cannot use effectively. Trans fats were not counted in the original Mediterranean diet considerations, as the limited amount of meat and dairy foods presented very few naturally occurring trans fats. They can be found in substantial quantities in today's processed foods such as cakes, biscuits, pastries, and fast foods. They are strongly related to the risk of heart disease in our modern diet, and no "safe" level of trans fat intake has been identified.

Dairy foods Traditionally high in fat, milk, cheese, and butter were taken in small quantities in the original Mediterranean diet. However, if adding years to your life is what you are aiming for, you need healthy bones too.

How do we reconcile the need for calcium-rich foods to maintain both healthy bones and heart, with the modest dairy-food intake of the Mediterranean style of eating? The answer is to choose low-fat dairy products, widely available today. Low-fat versions of foods preserve their calcium while reducing both total and saturated fat content.

An adult requires a minimum of 700mg calcium a day, an amount that can be met in three portions of dairy food. Around ¾ cup (180ml) milk, or a small carton of low-fat yogurt, or a matchbox-size piece (1 ounce/30g) of cheese constitutes a portion. In addition, dairy foods provide the vehicle in the UK for the addition of stanol or sterol esters, cholesterol-lowering plant extracts (see page 34). Stanol and sterol esters significantly reduce both total and LDL cholesterol levels.

Tofu, calcium-fortified soybean milks and juices, the bones of canned fish and green leafy vegetables are all good non-dairy calcium sources.

Meat and chicken Western-style meals place a large portion of meat firmly at the center of the meal, with vegetables and a carbohydrate as accompaniments. Meat is protein-rich but also contains saturated fat, and most of us eat more meat than is necessary to maintain health. A portion of meat, when cooked, should be approximately the same size as a deck of cards. A grilled pork chop (without fat and rind), a chicken breast, or two to three slices of roast meat are target amounts.

Remove visible fat before cooking (to avoid temptation later) and use a mono-unsaturated oil if frying. Meat and chicken lend themselves to food processing, often losing health benefits along the way. Roast chicken is much lower in calories and in total and saturated fat than chicken Kiev, and contains much less salt than processed chicken or turkey slices—so choose processed versions less often. Finally, you should try to alter the proportions of food on your plate so that the meat is the accompaniment to the vegetables, rather than the other way around.

Monounsaturated fats

Blood cholesterol levels are lowered when monounsaturated fat replaces saturated fat in the diet. Mono-unsaturated fats are less prone to oxidation, and this "stable" nature extends to their role in our body—helping to prevent the destabilizing of LDL cholesterol, and maintaining a neutral stance in the presence of background inflammation. For this reason they enhance the anti-inflammatory effects of omega-3 fish oils within the Mediterranean diet, in direct contrast to the omega-6-rich oils. The two main sources of monounsaturated fats in the Western diet are olive oil and modified rapeseed (canola) oil, (the latter is usually sold as "vegetable oil," but usually says on the label that it is made from rapeseed)

Cheese: percentage fat content and calorie load per serving

TYPE OF CHEESE	G FAT PER 100G (3½ OZ)	CALORIES PER 30G (1 OZ)
Cottage cheese	4	30
Ricotta cheese	11	43
Half-fat Cheddar/ hard cheese	15	82
Feta	20	75
Mozzarella	21	77
Camembert	23	87
Soybean cheese	27	96
Edam	25	102
Brie	27	103
Stilton	35	123
Parmesan	30	125
Cheddar	34	125
Cream cheese	48	132

Olive oil is the main fat source in the protective Mediterranean diet. Olive oil produced in the first pressing is called "extra virgin" olive oil, and is easily identified from its orange, yellow, or green color as derived from the native olive. The colors and flavors are important polyphenols—powerful plant antioxidants that confer additional heart-healthy benefits to this monounsaturated oil. As little as 1–2 tablespoons (15–30ml) of extra virgin olive oil daily brings significant health benefits.

Vegetable oil Rapeseed oil forms the basis of most blended vegetable oils, and is a cheap and healthy option for use in general cooking. Its neutral taste is preferred by some to the strong taste of olive oil, and its 10 percent omega-3 fat content makes it a useful alternative.

Polyunsaturated fats

Unlike other fat types, there are two "branches" of the polyunsaturated fatty acid family: the omega-6 and omega-3 polyunsaturated fats. The omega-6 family are found in corn, sunflower and soyabean oils, and polyunsaturated spreads, and provide the essential fatty acid linoleic acid. The omega-3 fatty acids are found in some seed oils (flaxseed and rapeseed), walnuts, and green, leafy vegetables; they provide the essential fatty acid alpha-linolenic acid (ALA). In turn, ALA can be converted by the body into the long-chain polyunsaturates, eicosopentanoic acid

(EPA) and docosohexanoic acid (DHA), but only 10–15 percent of ALA is usually converted. EPA and DHA are known as the "omega-3 fish oils," and eating oily fish gives you these fatty acids directly.

Omega-6 fats and omega-3 fats both reduce cholesterol levels, although omega-3 fats, particularly EPA and DHA, provide additional benefits for blood pressure and inflammation. Our diet generally provides an abundant omega-6 intake (from oils and spreads), but is inadequate in omega-3 fats due to their being present in relatively few foods. It is important to include both fish and plant sources of omega-3 fats in the diet in order to obtain sufficient to balance the effects of omega-6 fats.

From the 1980s, sunflower and corn oils and margarines (rich in omega-6 polyunsaturates) were considered a healthy, cholesterol-free alternative to butter and lard. In more recent years, however, a high intake of omega-6 fats has been shown to increase inflammation in the body, in contrast to the effects of the more "neutral" mono-unsaturated fats. Changing margarine and oil from polyunsaturated to mono-unsaturated has a beneficial effect on inflammation and artery health, and enhances the benefits of omega-3 fats in the body.

Oily fish Including oily fish in the diet is now recognized as being one of the most powerful tools in terms of diet for preventing heart disease. It has long been recognized that communities such as the

Inuit (groups living along the Arctic coast who eat fish regularly) have a much lower incidence of heart disease than non-fish eaters. Omega-3 fish oils, present in oily fish, seem to prevent potentially fatal disruption of heart rhythms, and reduce the risk of a blood clot (and the risk of a stroke, or heart attack), by thinning the blood and making it less sticky. They also reduce inflammation and stabilize the endothelium surface of the artery, protecting it from damage.

The amount required to gain these benefits is around 450mg of combined EPA and DHA daily, four times greater than the current average daily intake in the UK. This can be achieved by including two portions of fish per week, at least one of which should be oily (darker-fleshed fish). People who have already suffered a heart attack should aim to eat two to three portions of oily fish per week, yielding around 1000mg (1g) of EPA and DHA daily. Supplements may be required in order realistically to achieve this intake (see page 35).

Non-fish sources of omega-3 fats

There are other sources of omega-3 "fish oils," some naturally derived and some from fortified foods and drinks. Eggs from chickens fed a seed-rich diet can provide a useful amount of DHA, and their cholesterol content has a negligible effect on our blood cholesterol levels.

Oil-rich fish: omega-3 (EPA+DHA) content	MG OMEGA-3 PER PORTION
Mackerel	4500
Kipper	3700
Tuna—fresh	3000
Trout	2900
Salmon—fresh	2500
Herring (pickled)	2200
Pilchards—canned	1800
Salmon, canned	1400
Smoked salmon	1300
Mackerel—canned	1300
Sardines—canned	1200
Swordfish	1100
Crab—canned in brine	600
Cod	300
Tuna—canned	100

Non-fish sources of EPA and DHA	MG OMEGA-3 PER PORTION
Omega-3-enriched egg	500–750
Roast chicken, dark meat	330
Roast leg of lamb	240
Cheddar cheese	190
Whole milk	150
Roast chicken, light meat	130
Roast beef or pork	100
Omega-3-fortified margarines	75–160
Omega-3-fortified cow's milk	50–80
Omega-3-fortified fruit juices	70
Omega-3-enriched "shot" drinks	60–80
Egg	60

Plant sources of omega-3 (alpha linolenic acid)	MG ALA PER PORTION
Flaxseed and flaxseed oil (also known as linseed and linseed oil)	1800
Walnuts	1500
Walnut oil	1300
Rapeseed (canola) oil	1000
Soybean oil	800
Vegetable oil	700
Omega-3 fortified margarines	350
Baked beans	200
Spinach and green leafy vegetables	200
Groundnuts	200
Corn oil	100
Egg	60

Nuts (particularly walnuts) and seeds are rich in omega-3 fats. Smaller amounts occur naturally in green, leafy vegetables. Omega-3 fats are sometimes added to milks, margarines, orange juice, cereal bars, and bread, and these can contribute towards the recommended intake of 450mg or more a day, but remember to check the amount provided by a typical portion of these foods.

The plant version of omega-3, alpha-linolenic acid (ALA), can be converted in the body into EPA and DHA, but usually only 10–15 percent conversion is possible. ALA is beneficial to the body whether or not it is converted. Foods can contain both plant and fish oil versions of omega-3, such as eggs and fortified margarines.

Vegetarian diets

Vegetarianism covers the replacement of meat (and possibly fish and eggs) with pulses, nuts, seeds, and dairy products, through to the avoidance of any product derived from animal sources (known as veganism). Research has failed to show any clear benefits from following a vegetarian or vegan diet in terms of lowering cardiovascular risk, despite the lower blood pressure, lower blood cholesterol levels, and higher blood levels of antioxidant nutrients found in vegetarians compared to their meat-eating counterparts. Although total and LDL cholesterol levels are reduced with a vegetarian diet, the potential benefit is offset by a similar reduction in the cardioprotective HDL cholesterol levels.

Higher blood levels of the inflammatory protein homocysteine also commonly occur in vegetarians. Homocysteine is cleared from the body by processes requiring folic acid, vitamins B12 and B6. Vitamin B12 is found only in animal products and vegetarians have been shown to have low reserves of this nutrient, especially if they avoid milk, cheese, and eggs. It may be useful for strict vegetarians to include in their diet vitamin B12-fortified foods, such as some breakfast cereals, fortified margarines, and some vegetarian soybean products, or yeast extract (such as Marmite/Vegemite).

Use the food labeling guide on pages 39–41 to assess the healthiness of processed vegetarian products; e.g., some ranges of vegetarian burgers provide a higher level of total and saturated fat than their equivalent meat products.

Alcohol

Alcohol is a small but significant feature of the Mediterranean diet. A standard drink in the United States is any drink that contains about 14 grams of pure alcohol (about 0.6 fl oz).

Alcoholic drinks contain flavors and colors derived from the fruit or grain from which they originate and these can have some antioxidant potential (such as resveratrol in red wine), leading to the exhortation (by the French wine industry!) to choose red wine over other alcoholic drinks. However, it now appears to be the alcohol itself rather than its phytochemical content that influences health, and so any alcoholic beverage will have a similar effect.

So a small but regular alcohol intake brings a number of important benefits—reducing blood "stickiness," improving the action of insulin and, most important, helping to minimize the damage to the arteries that results from inflammation. Alcohol reduces LDL cholesterol and increases HDL cholesterol.

However, the benefits of alcohol are quickly lost at higher intakes, as alcohol is a toxin tolerable only in small quantities. A "safe" upper limit of alcohol intake for a man is 2 standard drinks a day with at least two alcohol-free days. For women, a safe upper limit is 1 drink a day with similar "rest" days. Unless you fall into any of the categories listed below, you can enjoy a daily drink as part of a healthy Mediterranean diet.

Understanding alcohol units

I UNIT OF ALCOHOL IS:

12 oz beer or cooler
1 glass (5 oz) of wine
1 single measure (1.5 oz) of
   spirits
1 small glass (3–4 oz) of fortified wine,
   such as sherry

Abstain from alcohol consumption if:

▸ You are underage.
▸ You have ever been assessed as being alcoholic, or have a family history of alcohol abuse.
▸ You have liver disease.
▸ You intend on driving, or could find yourself in a situation where you might have to operate heavy machinery.
▸ You have "alcohol-flushing" symptoms (where your skin turns red immediately after consuming alcohol).
▸ You are taking medication, either prescription or over-the-counter.
▸ You are pregnant or may be pregnant.

Supplements in the Heart-healthy Diet

Can the Mediterranean diet be improved by taking supplements? Many people take supplements in the belief that they are nutritional talismen, and there is some evidence that a "one-a-day" multivitamin and mineral supplement seems to be to some degree protective against cardiovascular disease, although the reason isn't fully known. It may be that a one-a-day supplement "tops up" any minor deficiencies in the diet. It could also be the case that supplement users tend to be more health conscious anyway and so they eat more healthily, do more exercise, and smoke less, making it difficult to separate the effects of their lifestyle as a whole from those of the supplements.

Apart from any possible "one-a-day" benefits, however, how do supplements in general measure up?

Niacin

Niacin (also known as nicotinic acid and vitamin B3) can increase HDL by 20–25 percent and maintains a healthy endothelium. Doctors may prescribe high-dose niacin, a much larger amount than would normally be available from diet alone. This level of niacin may cause "facial flushing," but starting with a low dose of 500mg a day can help to prevent this embarrassing side effect.

Iron

Iron is essential to prevent anemia, but it is also a highly reactive producer of free radicals, the cell-damaging chemicals produced as a by-product of our oxygen needs. Unless recommended by your doctor, iron supplements should be limited to no more than 100 percent of your recommended daily amount.

Antioxidant vitamins and minerals

LDL cholesterol can be easily oxidized, increasing the risk of atherosclerosis. Diets such as the Mediterranean diet, rich in dietary antioxidants, protect the body against cardiovascular disease and stroke. However, the use of dietary supplements containing high levels of the antioxidant vitamins A, C, and E does not provide the same benefits and may also reduce the effectiveness of the "statin" drugs prescribed to reduce blood cholesterol. A "one-a-day" multivitamin and mineral with a broad range of micronutrients around the 100 percent RDA level may be beneficial, but supplements that go beyond this level seem to offer no biological or health benefit.

Garlic

Garlic is of course a major flavoring in Mediterranean cookery, and population studies confirm that garlic consumption reduces cardiovascular risk. Garlic in the diet seems to protect LDL cholesterol from becoming unstable through oxidation, may reduce the "stickiness" of the blood and may help to moderate blood pressure. However, there is little consistent evidence to suggest that garlic supplements confer the same health benefits, and this is probably due to differences in extraction, tablet composition, and the level of any active ingredient within.

Stanol and sterol esters

Sterols are natural plant substances found in grains, vegetables, nuts, seeds, and pine tree extracts. When blended with fats they become sterol esters, also known as stanols, and have the ability to reduce LDL cholesterol by up to 20 percent while preserving HDL levels.

They work by blocking the uptake of dietary cholesterol and the re-uptake of cholesterol-rich bile salts that normally occurs in the bowel, increasing bile salt and cholesterol losses, and depleting the cholesterol "reserve." This is a dose-response effect, meaning that more ester confers more benefits, up to a plateau effect at around 2g a day, suggesting that this is the optimal dose. Stanol and sterol esters work best when taken with food, rather than alone.

In the UK, stanol and sterol esters are added to dairy products (although they are not naturally present in these foods), and mini "health drinks" (shot-size health drinks, available at supermarkets). In other countries they are added to fruit juices, cereals, chocolate, and grain bars. A portion of fortified dairy food (for example, ¾ cup milk, ¼–½ ounce margarine spread, or a single pot of yogurt) provides a third of the 2g dose. A single mini health drink provides the full

2g dose. There is no need to take one of these drinks alongside fortified foods, and you don't need to use them if your cholesterol is in the normal range.

Amount of stanol or sterol ester needed for effective load
▸ yogurt mini health drink each day *or*
▸ 3 portions of fortified foods: buttery/ olive/light margarine spreads, low-fat cream cheese spreads, single pot of low-fat yogurt, stanol-fortified milk

Fish oil
Fish oil supplements are popular for their omega-3 content, although the amount of "active" EPA and DHA they contain varies enormously. The minimum amount needed for "heart-friendly" benefits is 450mg EPA plus DHA daily. The traditional "teaspoon of cod liver oil" provides between 800 and 1400mg of EPA and DHA. Fish oil capsules contain much smaller amounts of EPA and DHA, as the capsule cannot hold more than 1ml (one-fifth of a teaspoon) of fish oil. Always read the label on supplements to check the amount of active fish oils present.

Note: Fish liver oils should not be taken in pregnancy without medical advice, as their vitamin A content is high.

Mediterranean Diet: A Lifestyle Approach

Healthy Eating for Lower Cholesterol provides the knowledge and ideas to help you take control of your cholesterol levels and protect your arteries from damage. Together with the lifestyle approach discussed earlier (see pages 20–33), adopting the "Mediterranean" style of eating will help you to get in shape, feel fitter, and lower your risk of heart disease and stroke.

This final section will consolidate the points discussed earlier in order to assist you in making healthy dietary choices whether you are eating out or at home.

The table below lists the top ten ways to "Mediterraneanize" your diet. Each of these has an independently beneficial effect on your blood's cholesterol level and artery health, so the more points you adopt as part of your diet, the greater the protective benefits will be. Rather than attempting to take on the whole plan in one go, that may prove over-ambitious, why not try addressing one new aspect each week? After all, control of your cholesterol requires a lifelong approach, and small steps, readily achieved, will form the foundation for a lifetime of good health. Within just ten weeks, your diet could be radically transformed for the better.

The top ten ways to "Mediterraneanize" your diet

1 Change to extra-virgin olive oil or vegetable (canola) oil, and margarines made from these (but use all fats and oils sparingly if you're overweight).

2 Include one to two portions of oily fish in your diet each week, or take a daily supplement providing at least 450–750mg of EPA plus DHA. Include other omega-3 rich foods each week.

3 Treat meat as a garnish, not the main component of a meal. An ideal portion is the size of a deck of cards (cooked weight). Fill the gaps on your plate with vegetables or salads.

4 Cook extra vegetables, or prepare side salads—you'll eat them. Keep frozen vegetables on standby as a quick, effortless, and nutritious way toward achieving your "five-a-day."

5 Choose wholegrain cereals and breads more often—at least once a day.

6 Eat more pulses. Beans on toast, or butterbean or lentil soups with wholegrain bread, are great snack meal ideas. Add lentils, beans, and peas to casseroles or serve as a side dish with the main course.

7 Have fruit, nuts, or seeds for between-meal snacks.

8 Use more herbs and spices in your cookery, for extra antioxidant nutrients.

9 Enjoy a glass of wine or a small beer most days.

10 Use low-fat dairy foods for calcium benefit without the saturated fat.

Maintain a healthy weight for your height

Your body weight reflects the overall balance between your energy input (from food and drink) and energy output (for your body's needs, plus extra for physical activity). Being overweight reduces the impact of any healthy changes on cholesterol management. Check your waist-to-hip ratio (WHR) to see if you need to lose weight (see page 18). Following the advice in this book will help you to redress your energy balance and, in turn, to maintain a healthier weight.

Plan to eat regularly

"Plan" is the key word here. In our busy 24/7 lifestyle, what we choose to eat is often relegated to second place behind other, seemingly more important matters. We end up snacking on whatever comes to hand, be it chocolate, crisps, cakes or cookies, none of which is conducive to cholesterol control. If you plan what you're eating, however, you will find that you can improve the nutritional value of your diet.

Breakfast

Get up ten minutes earlier in the morning to make time for breakfast—it boosts your metabolic rate and also your mental acuity. Best choices include:

▸ wholegrain cereals with 1% or 2% milk

▸ whole wheat or granary toast with an olive-oil spread and yeast extract or reduced-sugar jelly or marmalade.

▸ a breakfast kipper, mackerel, or an omega-3-enriched boiled or poached egg with whole wheat toast, if you have time!

▸ a whole wheat or oat-based cereal bar

(with the main ingredient being the grain, and containing less than 10g/½ ounce of sugar per bar) with a drinking yogurt or ready-made low-fat yogurt smoothie if time is short

It's also a good idea to have fresh or dried fruit, or a glass of fruit juice to make a start on your "five-a-day."

Lunch

Having a snack lunch? Best option is to take a sandwich from home, and use an ice pack if there is no fridge in your workplace. Use whole wheat or granary bread and rolls or the higher-fiber white bread spread with low-fat or mono-unsaturated-rich margarines. Great fillings include:
▸ canned tuna (in brine or water) with low-calorie mayo and cucumber
▸ fresh or canned salmon with salad
▸ omega-3-enriched hard-cooked egg with tomato
▸ cottage cheese or low-fat soft cheese (such as ricotta) with chopped scallions and mixed herbs
▸ chicken or lean meat with salad.

Other good quick lunch options include:
▸ vegetable soup and a wholegrain roll
▸ baked beans or low-fat hummous with toast

▸ rice or pasta salad with plenty of vegetables and lean meat or oily fish.

If you need a snack to finish your meal, choose from the list below. Snacking is a way of life, but it can be made healthier so that you need not feel deprived when all around you are eating:
▸ Healthiest options: fresh fruit and raw vegetables such as crudités; rice cakes.
▸ Moderate-calorie snacks: a handful of nuts or seeds; lower-fat crisps; unsalted popcorn; dried-fruit "snack packs";

baked wheat or rice-based snacks.
▸ Substantial (but healthy) snacks: fruit scones; whole wheat muffins; oatcakes; whole wheat pita breads with lower-fat dips, such as reduced-fat hummous, or yogurt-based dips like tzatziki.

Main meal

Your main meal of the day is the cornerstone of healthy eating, and if you have children you can use this meal to give them a sound basis for lifelong healthy eating habits. If you're a "heat and

serve" cook, you should aim to cook a meal from basic ingredients once a week to start with, then build on this until at least half of your meals each week are cooked from scratch. Refer to the top ten Mediterranean ways (see page 37) as well as the tips that follow to ensure that your main meal is healthy.

Saucepans and skillets Your cookware can help you to eat more healthily—if you use non-stick pans you can cook your food without added fat. Any way of cooking is better than frying. Steam, boil, poach, grill, or barbecue foods instead. Griddles, grilling, and broiling machines allow the fat to drain away from meat and fatty products. Cook roast meats on a trivet to allow the fat to run off. A non-stick wok can be used for healthy, stir-fried meals using a little oil, stock, or wine.

Beans and lentils For casseroles and stews, use less meat and add pulses to improve the nutritional profile of the meal. Add canned beans and extra vegetables for healthier versions with texture, or lentils for a "hidden" source of fiber and other plant benefits if family members don't like beans.

Dried lentils, peas, and beans are a cheap and healthy way to improve your diet but need to be cooked according to the instructions on the packet to remove harmful substances, making them a slow addition to any meal. Cook large quantities of dried pulses, then freeze in smaller portions for convenience. You can then defrost in the microwave as needed or add straight to a casserole, suspending the cooking time until the frozen pulses have thawed. Alternatively, use the canned versions that are "ready to go."

Salads Use any fruits and vegetables you like. Prepare while a microwave meal is cooking, or serve salad "on the side" to accompany. A breakfast bowl of salad as a starter is a proven way to help lose weight, by blunting your appetite for the main course. Instead of mayonnaise or full-fat salad dressings, use an oil "spray" dressing with vinegar or lemon juice and herbs, or a low-calorie version of salad dressing.

Pastry Avoid pastry of any type—it's 50 percent fat by weight. For savory dishes, substitute potato topping, or lasagne sheets instead of a pastry base. For desserts, cut out the pastry completely. Lemon meringue tastes just as light and refreshing a dessert without the "pie" base. If you are out, choose a baguette and soup rather than a hot pasty.

Salt Most of us take between 8 and 12g of salt a day, although the safe limit for adults is actually 6g a day. Having said that, most salt in the diet comes from processed foods rather than being added at mealtimes, so home-cooked meals can significantly lower salt intake. It's essential for people with high blood pressure to cut down on salt to reduce the risk of heart attack or stroke. Sea salt, organic, rock, and flavored salts are all salt (sodium chloride), so should be avoided. Avoid adding salt to foods, but use a low-salt substitute if you need to. Herbs and spices make great alternative flavors. Compare food labels to choose lower-salt alternatives.

To convert the sodium content of a food into the amount of salt present, multiply by 2.5: that is, 0.6g sodium = 0.6 x 2.5 = 1.5g salt.

Food labeling

In the real world, we often don't have the time to make every meal. Being able to "read" food labels will help you to make great choices—in terms of comparing the nutritional benefits of different foods, and also in working out how they fit into your diet.

The good news is that it is now common for almost all food packaging to carry information about the product

A guide to assessing the information on food labels	
THIS IS A LOT, PER 100G	THIS IS A LITTLE, PER 100G
20g fat	3g fat
3g saturated fat	1g saturated fat
10g sugar	2g sugar
0.5g sodium/ 1.25g salt	0.1g sodium/ 0.25g salt
3g fibre	0.5g fibre

Sample food label: macaroni and cheese for two

Serving Size	1 cup (228g)	Calories	250
Servings Per Container	2	Calories from Fat	110

INGREDIENT	AMOUNT PER SERVING	
Total fat:	12g	18%
Saturated Fat	3g	15%
Trans Fat	3g	
Cholesterol	30mg	10%
Sodium	470mg	20%
Total Carbohydrate:	31g	10%
Dietary Fiber	0g	0%
Sugars	5g	
Protein	5g	
Vitamin A		4%
Vitamin C		2%
Calcium		20%
Iron		4%

% daily values for a macaroni and cheese meal

AMOUNT PER MEAL	DV E.G. FOR WOMEN	% DV FROM MEAL
250 calories	2000 calories	10%
12g fat	65g fat	18%
20g saturated fat	20g saturated fat	15%
30mg cholesterol	300mg cholesterol	10%
.47g sodium	2.4g sodium	20%
31g total carb	300g total carb	10%
0g dietary fiber	30g dietary fiber	0%

Guideline daily values (DVs)

NUTRIENT	MEN	WOMEN
Energy (kcal)	2500	2000
Fat (g)	85	65
Sat Fat (g)	25	20
Cholesterol (mg)	300	300
Sodium (g)	2.4	2.4
Total Carb (g)	375	300
Dietary Fiber (g)	30g	25g

inside and to include most of the essential facts—serving size, calories and nutritional information. Here's a crash course in decoding the key.

First take a look at the serving size and the number of servings in the package. This should be at the top of the label and listed in familiar units, such as cups or pieces, followed by the metric amount e.g., 228g. Then look at the size of the package and ask yourself, "How many servings am I consuming?" In the sample label, one serving of macaroni and cheese equals one cup. Therefore if you ate the whole container, you would eat two cups and dramatically alter the nutritional impact of this meal.

For example, one serving of macaroni and cheese contains 250 calories, but if you ate two, this would double. As a general guide, 40 calories is considered low, 100 moderate and anything above 400 high, so you could very easily find yourself consuming far more calories than you need and putting on weight accordingly.

Most people are aware of calories and can easily keep an eye on their recommended daily allowance. However, it is difficult to remember all the statistics that relate to the key nutrients and so always have the % Daily Values column as your indispensable frame of reference. It is used by all food manufacturers and retailers and is based on the predicted needs of an average person eating a healthy diet (see the Guideline Daily Values table). All the math has been done for you and lets you know if the meal you are eating contains healthy levels of dietary fiber or your whole daily allowance of carbohydrate!

The nutrients in the list can be divided into two groups. The first group, consisting of fat, saturated fat, trans fat, cholesterol and sodium are the ones we generally eat in adequate amounts and should try to limit as part of a healthy diet. Therefore, if you look at the guideline daily value table, the amount listed here is the upper limit of what you should look to consume in one day. However, in contrast, most people don't get enough dietary fiber, vitamin A, vitamin C, calcium, and iron in their diets and so the guideline daily value here is the minimum you should incorporate into your meals to improve your health and help reduce the risk of some diseases and conditions.

Try to get into the habit of comparing one or two favorite foods each week with guideline values and choose the healthier options accordingly. Make a particular effort to minimize salt intake and look for foods that are low in saturated fats, trans fats, and cholesterol in order to support a heart healthy lifestyle.

Eating out: healthy choices

Eating out is an enjoyment, both for the social experience and for the novelty of trying foods that you may not have eaten before. The temptation is often to go for those foods that are too complex to attempt at home, but these tend to be the higher-fat, higher-calorie menu choices —and there's no food labeling to help you choose wisely.

If you eat out occasionally, enjoy your meal, drink a modest amount of alcohol and indulge. If, however, you eat out regularly—say, more than twice a week—you need to factor in health when making your choice so that you do not abandon an otherwise healthy diet.

The "Mediterranean" way can be factored into any style of cuisine—as Dan's recipes in this book demonstrate. Your goal when eating out should simply be to select dishes with a high vegetable or salad content, served with a modest amount of meat or vegetarian equivalent, in a non-fatty sauce. Here are some tips:

▸ Choose a vegetable soup, fruit, or salad

appetizer—low-calorie and nutrient-packed. Have some bread (preferably brown), but use it to mop up the soup or dressing and don't add butter.

▶ For the main course, consider how your plate should look: that is, loaded with vegetables, with meat on the side. Feel free to say "yes" to more vegetables, and a side salad will improve vegetable intake further still. Ask for olive oil, lemon juice, or oil-free dressing instead of full-fat mayonnaise for the salad.

▶ Choose low-fat carbohydrates as a sound meal base. Boiled or baked potatoes are better than either wedges, roast potatoes, or French fries. Boiled or steamed rice is better than fried or pilau rice. Boiled noodles and pasta make a sound base.

▶ As a rule of thumb, go for the dish with the least sauce or fried ingredients – a grilled fish dish, lean steak, or chicken, or meat in a tomato-based sauce are good choices.

Foods from around the world

Greek Start with Greek or tomato salad (light on the dressing) or choose tzatziki (yogurt and cucumber appetizer) with bread. For the main course, try to avoid dishes like moussaka—these are rich in oil, cream, and cheese. Also limit your intake of fat-rich phyllo pastry—either savory (as in spanakopita) or sweet (baklava). Select foods such as stuffed vine leaves (dolmades), roasted meats, or meat kebabs, served with couscous, boiled rice, or pita breads, or plaki (fish cooked in a tomato-based sauce). Choose fruit for your dessert.

Indian Traditional Indian (south Asian) meals are heavy on the oil—used to release the flavors from herbs and spices before other ingredients are added. Avoid the highest-fat options when eating out —coconut-flavored curries such as korma are high in total and saturated fats. Pakoras and bhaji are usually deep-fried, as are samosas. Fried breads (like paratha and puri) and stuffed breads (keema nan) are also highly calorific and loaded with fat. Choose instead a limited number of poppadums or papads for your appetizer, with tandoori- or tikka-style meats, or tomato and onion-based sauces. Include some dahl—Indian cookery lends itself to using beans, lentils, and garbanzo beans, and these are all good sources of fiber.

Choose plain, boiled rice rather than pilau and dosai or plain naan rather than filled varieties (keema and peshwari naan). Allow vegetable dishes to cool for a few minutes, then skim the oil layer from the surface and discard it, leaving the healthier vegetables below. Avoid ordering too many dishes, or share with a friend. Traditional Indian sweets are high in fat and sugar, so rather than the Indian ice-cream menu, go for the sorbet option or a fruit salad as low-fat alternatives.

If you are cooking Indian at home, try steam-frying the spices to release their aroma and flavor: use half the amount of oil that you would normally use to fry herbs and spices, and if they become too dry during cooking, add a splash or two of boiling water (hence the term "steam-fry"). This will release the flavors without excessive fat or calorie load. You can add further water if you need to. Use canned garbanzo beans, lentils, or other pulses to boost the cholesterol-lowering effect of the vegetables.

If you are buying Indian to eat in, always choose the supermarket "healthier option" to keep the total fat intake down. Skip the onion bhaji, samosa, or pakora as a side dish and choose vegetables cooked with spices in a tomato-sauce base for a healthier option, or a side salad to keep to your five-a-day goal.

Chinese Avoid the fried spring rolls, and any other fried dishes. Wontons (steamed dumplings), boiled or steamed rice, and noodles should form the base of the meal. Stir-fried and vegetable dishes are better choices than deep-fried dishes such as sweet-'n'-sour balls, pancake rolls, and prawn crackers.

Italian Italian food is often considered to epitomize Mediterranean cookery, but you should still be cautious about some aspects of Italian cuisine! Choose soup, salad, fish, or roasted vegetables for an appetizer, and pasta in a tomato- or clam-based sauce for the main course. If you fancy pizza, the thin-crust type is the least calorific, and toppings such as ham, chicken, vegetable, tuna, or seafood tend to be the lowest in calories. Enjoy a side salad, but if you are overweight, do not mop up olive oil with the bread side dish

—a sure way to add 150 calories to your meal! Avoid "filled" pastas such as cheese-filled cannelloni or meat lasagne, pasta with butter or cream, fried calamari and other fish, and Italian pastries. Choose a fruit-based dessert or sorbets rather than gâteaux or ice cream for dessert.

French Traditional French cooking uses high-fat sauces and cooking methods whereas nouvelle cuisine is more healthful by virtue of its small portion sizes. Choose meat or fish in a wine- or vegetable-based sauce, rather than in a hollandaise, mornay, bechamel, or bearnaise sauce. Avoid "au gratin" potato dishes for their high-saturated-fat cheese and cream content. Choose fruit-based desserts like oranges in Grand Marnier, or fruit salad, or meringue-based desserts rather than traditional tortes, tatins, and crème caramel.

Mexican Mexican cuisine is perhaps one of the least compatible with controlling cholesterol. Heavily meat-based, it uses a variety of high-fat ingredients to create the complex hot-with-cool flavors and this makes it difficult to choose healthily. The best choices are chicken fajitas, chicken or beef enchiladas, and salads. Salsa is a tomato-based healthy dip, and guacamole—made from avocado—is a healthy but high-calorie option. Keep the nachos to nibble to a scant handful—it's amazing just how many can be eaten before a meal. Corn tortillas are lower in fat than flour tortillas. The high-fat foods to avoid where possible include sour cream and grated cheeses, refried beans, chorizo sausage, and flour tortillas such as quesadillas, chimichangas, and burritos.

Fast food Avoid French fries—but if you really can't resist, limit your intake.

Choose the smallest burger or chicken grill, and don't go for added cheese or relishes. Choose tea, coffee, water, fruit juice, diet drinks, or milk instead of high-sugar drinks and high-fat milkshakes. Do not eat the batter on fried fish and add some vegetables, such as peas, baked beans or pickled onions.

Or take inspiration from Dan's recipes—and eat in instead!

From the Chef

I specialize in healthy eating and always want to make it fresh, easy, and interesting. I have been very lucky to work in many countries across Asia and Europe. The Mediterranean is a huge inspiration and, wonderfully, this style of cooking is recognized as being one of the most healthy too. I have included lots of simple and delicious fish recipes, that I hope will inspire those who are unused to cooking with fish. I like to use ingredients that are easy to find, as well as experimenting with new ideas, but I do not try to "re-invent the wheel" as there are so many dishes out there that are classic and do not need change. Presentation is important and I enjoy creating dishes that appeal to the eye as well as the tastebuds.

It is vital to keep cholesterol under control, and happily a balanced diet can make a real difference. In this book I hope you will see foods you love, want to make the dishes and not feel that you are compromising on flavor by not eating foods high in saturated fats. After losing weight myself I never use butter or cream in my recipes, but I never feel deprived. Think not only of olive oil but also of other interesting oils that are low in saturated fat, like sesame oil and walnut oil. Fresh herbs and spices are also a great way to liven up the simplest of dishes, from basil and mint to ginger, chile, and lemongrass; you will see how you can get food to explode with flavor and then you will never miss the fat.

Always try to fuel your body with the right things and you will instantly feel the benefit. If it can be done in a tasty, easy way I think you will be halfway there!

1 Breakfasts and Brunches

More than granola
This recipe is for homemade granola but you could substitute ready-made granola and add the maple syrup, milk, and yogurt. Perfect for a Sunday brunch, served in large wine glasses. **Serves 4–6**

2 cups jumbo porridge oats
½ cup flaked bran or wheat germ
1½ cups barley or rye flakes
½ cup hazelnuts, lightly crushed
½ cup slivered almonds
⅓ cup raisins
2 oz dried apricots, chopped
4–6 tablespoons maple syrup
4–5 tablespoons 2% milk
4 tablespoons low-fat Greek yogurt

Mix all the ingredients together well in a large mixing bowl. Refrigerate overnight. (You may need to add more milk to keep the right consistency as the granola absorbs most of the liquid.)
Those with a sweet tooth may want to top with more maple syrup!

Per serving: 547 calories, 20.4g fat, 2.5g saturated fat, 0.04g sodium

Energizer smoothie
The perfect breakfast for people on the go. Make it the night before and take it with you to work; it will fill you up and give you a steady supply of energy throughout the morning. **Serves 4**

2 bananas
1¼ cups 1% milk
⅔ cup fresh orange juice
1 cup low-fat yogurt
⅔ cup fresh strawberries
1 tablespoon honey
1 teaspoon ground cinnamon
4 passion fruit

Well, not too much to this one—just put all the ingredients except the passion fruit in a blender and whizz until smooth.
When ready to serve just spoon some passion fruit seeds over the top.
This can be kept in the fridge for at least a day, so make the night before to have on hand the next morning. Another tip is to use fruit that is about to "turn"—it works well and is a great way to avoid wasting expensive fruit.

Per serving: 154 calories, 1.1g fat, 0.6g saturated fat, 0.09g sodium

Buckwheat pancakes
These are pancakes but made with buckwheat flour, that has a delicious flavor. Try adding fresh fruit to the batter for extra sweetness. **Serves 4–6**

1¼ cups buckwheat flour
2 teaspoons brown sugar
1 teaspoon baking powder
4 eggs
2 cups 1% milk

2 tablespoons vegetable
    (canola) oil
Fresh fruit and maple syrup
    to serve

Mix together in a large bowl the flour, sugar, and baking powder.
Now crack in the eggs and add the milk. Whisk with a hand whisk until smooth.
Heat some of the oil in a skillet over a medium heat.
Drop a generous tablespoon of the batter into the skillet and cook until bubbles appear (around 2 minutes), then flip over and cook for a further 30 seconds. Repeat with the remaining oil and batter.
Serve the pancakes with fresh fruit and maple syrup.

Per serving: 326 calories, 12g fat, 2.1g saturated fat, 0.27g sodium

Breakfast bars
These make a great start to the day, especially if you need breakfast on the go. Bake ahead of time and take with you to work. You can use any combination of dried fruit, nuts, and seeds. **Makes 22–24**

½ cup dried figs
½ cup dried apricots
½ cup dried pears
⅓ cup sunflower seeds
½ cup cashew nuts

⅓ cup porridge oats
½ cup whole wheat flour
¼ cup fresh orange juice
3 tablespoons runny honey

Preheat the oven to 375°F. Grease an 8-inch square shallow baking tray.
Place the fruit in a blender and blend until roughly chopped.
Add the sunflower seeds, cashew nuts, oats, and flour and mix in well but do not blend.
Now add the juice and honey and blend roughly. Transfer the mix into the baking tray and bake in the oven for 20–25 minutes or until golden brown.
Take out of the oven and allow to cool before slicing into bars.

Per bar: 79 calories, 2.8g fat, 0.4g saturated fat, 0.01g sodium

Banana oatmeal *Porridge is good with any fruit, but if you put bananas at the bottom of the bowl the porridge warms them—lovely on a cold winter morning! You can use any toasted seeds for the topping.* **Serves 4**

2 bananas, sliced
1¼ cups rolled oats
1–1¼ cups 2% milk

2–3 tablespoons maple syrup
  or runny honey
2 tablespoons sunflower seeds,
  toasted in a dry skillet

Divide the banana slices between 4 small bowls.
Place the oats and milk in a saucepan, mix well and bring to a boil. Stir as the oatmeal thickens. After about 5 minutes, when the porridge has thickened, pour into serving bowls.
Drizzle with maple syrup or honey and serve sprinkled with the sunflower seeds.

Per serving: 238 calories, 6.2g fat, 1.4g saturated fat, 0.03g sodium

Scrambled eggs and smoked salmon *There is nothing quite like wild salmon from Scottish or Atlantic waters, and the fact it is good for you makes it better still!* **Serves 4**

6 eggs plus 2 egg whites
Drizzle of vegetable
  (canola) oil

1 lb Scottish smoked salmon
Bunch of fresh chives, chopped

In a large bowl whisk together the eggs and the egg whites.
Heat a drizzle of oil in a large non-stick pan. Add the eggs and cook on a medium-low heat, gently and continuously pulling them into the centre of the pan. This allows the eggs to cook without burning.
Remove from the heat when the eggs are still a little runny as they will continue to cook with the heat of the pan and you do not want to overcook them.
Serve with smoked salmon and chopped chives.

Per serving: 291 calories, 14.7g fat, 3.7g saturated fat, 2.25g sodium

Corn patties with dipping sauce

Perfect for a Sunday brunch. Serve with Thai dipping sauce for an Eastern twist, or alternatively with salsa to give a Mexican flavor.

Serves 4–6

18 oz canned sweetcorn, drained
1 small onion
1 egg plus 1 egg white
Handful of fresh cilantro, plus
   extra to garnish
1¼ cups all-purpose flour
1 teaspoon baking powder

Freshly ground black pepper
2 tablespoons vegetable
   (canola) oil for frying
Thai dipping sauce or salsa
   (see page 135), to serve

Put all the ingredients (except for 3½ oz of the corn and the oil) in a blender and blend until smooth.

Mix the remaining corn in by hand.

Heat the oil in a skillet.

Form large spoonfuls of the mix into patties and fry, 4 at a time, cooking for 2 minutes on each side.

Transfer to a serving plate, garnish with cilantro and serve the Thai dipping sauce or salsa on the side.

Per serving (without dipping sauce): 311 calories, 8.6g fat, 1g saturated fat, 0.46g sodium

Mexican breakfast burrito

Here is a Mexican recipe fit for any weekend brunch; it's always a winner when you need something filling and satisfying. It's easy to prepare ahead of time and can be served at room temperature. **Serves 4**

14 oz can refried beans
4 large flour tortillas
2 cups reduced-fat Cheddar cheese, shredded
½ cup low-fat fromage frais
2 tablespoons 2% milk
1 small red chile, finely chopped
Freshly ground black pepper
1 tablespoon vegetable (canola) oil

Preheat the oven to 400°F.

Drain the beans and mash them.

Put each tortilla on a large sheet of foil, spread with the mashed beans and add the cheese. Fold the foil over the top and seal, keeping it flat, then put in the oven and cook for 8–10 minutes. Remove from the oven and set aside.

Mix the fromage frais, milk, and chilli in a bowl and season with black pepper.

Open the foil parcels and spoon the fromage frais mixture on top of the burritos, dividing it equally between them.

This can also be served with salsa or tofu guacamole (see page 135).

Per serving: 381 calories, 19.1g fat, 8.7g saturated fat, 0.93g sodium

Congee

This dish is eaten all over Asia. It's perfect to start the day with (especially when the weather is cold) as the rice releases energy slowly through the morning. Steamed chicken may be added for a more filling dish. **Serves 4–6**

2½–2¾ quarts vegetable broth, homemade (see page 138) or made with low-salt stock cubes
1½ cups white rice (short-grain is perfect)
1 cup water
2 hard-cooked eggs, quartered
6 scallions, very finely chopped
2 tablespoons reduced-salt soy sauce

Put the stock in a pan and bring to the boil.

Rinse the rice in a sieve to wash away any starch, then add to the stock, lowering the heat to a gentle simmer. Cook for 1 hour, adding the water about 20 minutes into the cooking time. Stir a few times throughout the cooking time, adding more water if needed.

Spoon into soup bowls and add a couple of egg quarters, chopped spring onions, and a drizzle of soy sauce to each one.

Per serving: 403 calories, 4.6g fat, 0.8g saturated fat, 0.65g sodium

Dried fruit muffins
Any dried fruits will work, from raisins to apricots. You could also try adding a mixture of nuts to the batter. Serve with freshly squeezed orange juice and enjoy! **Serves 4 (makes about 12 muffins)**

1 teaspoon vegetable (canola) oil	4 tablespoons whole wheat flour
8 tablepoons caster sugar	2 eggs
2 cups mixed dried fruit	⅔ cup 2% milk

Preheat the oven to 375°F. Grease 12 muffin moulds with vegetable oil.

Heat 6 tablespoons of caster sugar in a heavy-based saucepan until it dissolves. Add the dried fruit, stir in and set aside.

Place the flour and remaining sugar into a bowl. Whisk in the eggs and then add the milk, whisking to form a thick batter.

Pour the batter into the pan with the dried fruit and sugar mix, then divide among the muffin moulds. Bake in the oven for 10–15 minutes.

Allow to cool and serve.

Per muffin: 121 calories, 1.6g fat, 0.4g saturated fat, 0.03g sodium

Spanish omelet
This is an easy dish to make. If you have any left over, keep in the fridge and save for later—it is good cold as well as hot. Add a variety of whatever vegetables are in season, to suit your own taste. **Serves 6**

2 tablespoons olive oil or vegetable (canola) oil, plus extra for greasing	1 large onion, thinly sliced
3 large potatoes, very thinly sliced	6 eggs
	½ teaspoon paprika
	Freshly ground black pepper
	Dash of Tabasco sauce

Preheat the oven to 300°F. Use the oil to grease an 8 x 12 inch baking tray.

Heat the oil in a large skillet and cook the potatoes until nearly soft, then add the onion and cook until it is transparent. Turn into a large bowl and set aside to cool.

Lightly beat the eggs and pour over the potatoes and onion. Add the paprika, pepper, and Tabasco sauce and mix well.

Tip the mixture into the baking tray and cook in the oven for about 35 minutes until the centre is cooked (it should wobble when shaken). Alternatively, if your skillet has an ovenproof handle, pour the mixture back into the skillet, cook for a few minutes over a low heat, then place in the oven for 30 minutes.

Cut into pizza-style wedges and serve.

Per serving: 202 calories, 10.1g fat, 2.1g saturated fat, 0.08g sodium

Steamed dim sum
Dim sum is a traditional Sunday breakfast all across China. It's actually very easy to make, so why not give it a go? For a vegetarian version, use cabbage, mushrooms and water chestnuts instead of meat. **Serves 8–10**

1 lb lean ground chicken
1 lb lean ground pork
1 egg white
1 tablespoon reduced-salt soy
   sauce, plus extra for dipping

2 garlic cloves
1 inch cube fresh ginger root
1 tablespoon sesame oil
5 scallions, finely chopped
1–2 packs won ton wrappers

Put all the ingredients apart from the scallions and won ton wrappers in a food processor. Blend to a rough paste.

Add the chopped scallions.

Now take a won ton sheet and place a tablespoon of the mixture on to the centre. Moisten the edges with water and crimp them all the way round, making an open parcel. Repeat with the rest of the wrappers and mixture. (You could also try crimping the edges to make closed parcels.)

Put the parcels in a single or double steamer (or a bamboo steamer) and steam for 8–10 minutes.

Serve with soy sauce.

Per serving: 222 calories, 5.8g fat, 1.7g saturated fat, 0.36g sodium

Fresh salmon kedgeree
A traditional breakfast simplified and with much of the fat removed. Salmon adds a milder flavor to this dish than traditional kippers, but still provides the healthy omega-3 fats. **Serves 4**

1 tablespoon vegetable
   (canola) oil
1 large onion, finely chopped
2 garlic cloves, crushed
2 lbs cooked white rice (any
   rice will work with this)
Water and vinegar, for cooking
   the eggs

4 eggs
18 oz fresh salmon fillet
Dash of paprika
Freshly ground black pepper
Handful of fresh parsley,
   chopped

In a large pan or wok, heat the oil and add the onion. Cook on a medium heat for 5 minutes, trying not to let the onion brown. Add the garlic, then the rice and toss well. Remove from the heat.

Meanwhile, in a pan, heat two thirds water to one third vinegar (white wine or rice vinegar is best). When it is boiling hard add 2 of the eggs and poach for 2 minutes. Remove from the pan and add to a bowl of cold water to stop the cooking process. Repeat with the remaining 2 eggs.

Heat a non-stick pan and add the salmon. You don't need oil when cooking salmon in a non-stick pan as it releases its own oils. Cook over a medium heat for 3–4 minutes on each side.

Return the rice pan to the heat and add the salmon to it, flaking it as you mix it in well with the rice mixture.

Add paprika and freshly ground pepper to taste.

Remove from the heat after a minute or so and mix in the parsley.

Divide the mixture between 4 bowls, placing a poached egg on each, and serve.

Per serving: 654 calories, 23.1g fat, 4.5g saturated fat, 0.13g sodium

Soups and Salads

2

Butternut squash soup *The butternut has such a rich flavor that you end up with a filling soup and a silky texture even without the oil, butter, or cream that is so often used in soups.* **Serves 4–6**

1 medium butternut squash
1 tablespoon olive oil
1 onion, diced
1 small potato, quartered
2 garlic cloves
Salt and freshly ground black
   pepper

1½ pints vegetable broth,
   homemade (see page 138)
   or made with low-salt
   stock cubes
Handful of chives, chopped

Peel the butternut squash, scoop out the seeds and cut the flesh into thick wedges.

Heat the oil in a large saucepan, then add the onion and cook on a low heat for 1–2 minutes.

Add the butternut and potato and coat in the oil. Cook for 2 minutes on a medium heat. Add the garlic and season.

Now add the broth and simmer for 25 minutes.

Using a hand blender or food processor, blend thoroughly.

To serve, sprinkle with some chopped chives.

Per serving: 168 calories, 3.3g fat, 0.4g saturated fat, 0.27g sodium

Chilled avocado soup

Avocados are rich in healthier monounsaturated fat. This yummy soup can also be made into a dipping sauce for asparagus or artichokes (use 3 tablespoons of broth per each half avocado). **Serves 4**

4 slices bacon
2 ripe avocados
2½ pints vegetable or chicken broth, homemade (see pages 138 and 139) or made with low-salt stock cubes
2 tablespoons plain low-fat yogurt
Juice of ½ lemon
Freshly ground black pepper

Remove all the fat from the bacon slices—I do this with scissors—and cut the bacon into thin strips. Fry in a skillet on a medium heat until brown.

Meanwhile, in a blender, whizz the avocados, broth, yogurt and lemon juice until smooth and season with black pepper.

Serve chilled, or at room temperature, garnished with the strips of bacon.

Per serving: 220 calories, 14.1g fat, 2g saturated fat, 0.56g sodium

Corn and lemongrass soup
Lemongrass is widely used in Thai cuisine and has a lemony aroma. This soup is easy to make and can be kept for up to a week in the fridge.

Serves 8

10–12 lemongrass stalks
8–10 corn cobs
2 tablespoons vegetable (canola) oil
1 large onion, finely chopped
1 garlic clove, crushed

4 pints vegetable broth, homemade (see page 138) or made with low-salt stock cubes
Handful of fresh chives, chopped

Peel the lemongrass stalks until you get to the tender white parts that are easy to cut without fraying. Now finely chop them and set aside.

Using a knife, slice the corn kernels off the cobs and put in a bowl, reserving 3 tablespoons of kernels for garnishing.

Heat the oil in a large saucepan and add the onion, cooking for 2–3 minutes. Add the prepared lemongrass, crushed garlic, and bowl of corn kernels. Stir for a minute and add the broth. Simmer for 20–25 minutes on a low heat.

Meanwhile, heat a skillet with a drizzle of olive oil and fry the reserved corn kernels for a few minutes until crispy and golden brown.

When the soup is ready, put in a blender and whizz until smooth.

Serve topped with a few fried corn kernels and a sprinkling of chopped chives.

Per serving: 187 calories, 4.9g fat, 0.2g saturated fat, 0.15g sodium

Gazpacho
A Spanish classic that you do not always see on a menu these days, that is a shame. It gets better over time, so keep in the fridge for a few days. Delicious on a spring or summer day. **Serves 4–6**

Handful each of:
  fresh chives
  fresh tarragon
  fresh parsley
  fresh basil
  fresh marjoram
2 garlic cloves, crushed
1 red bell pepper, diced
4 large tomatoes, peeled, seeded, and diced

Juice of 1 lemon
3/4 pint vegetable broth, made with a low-salt stock cube, cooled
1/4 pint tomato juice
1 onion, finely chopped
1 small red chile
1/2 cucumber, finely chopped
Freshly ground black pepper

Chop the herbs and mix with the crushed garlic.

Add the red pepper and tomatoes to the herbs and also the lemon juice.

Add the cold broth and the tomato juice.

Add the onion, red chile and cucumber to the soup.

Season with black pepper and chill for at least 4 hours before serving.

Per serving: 67 calories, 0.9g fat, 0.1g saturated fat, 0.12g sodium

Hearty fish soup
Try this with any fish and add seafood if you wish. There really are no boundaries as every kind of fish and seafood will work. Very warming on a winter's day.

Serves 6–8

1–2 tablespoons olive oil
1 garlic clove, crushed
1½ pints fish broth, homemade (see page 139), or made with low-salt stock cubes
8 oz halibut, roughly chopped
8 oz cod, roughly chopped

8 oz swordfish, roughly chopped
8 small scallops
6 medium tomatoes, quartered
1 tablespoon tomato pureé
Handful of fresh chives, chopped
4 scallions, sliced

Heat the oil in a large saucepan on a medium heat, throw in the garlic and turn for 30 seconds.
Add the broth, followed by all the fish, the tomatoes, and tomato pureé and boil for 5–8 minutes. It's that simple!
Serve garnished with chopped chives and sliced scallions.

Per serving: 193 calories, 5.2g fat, 0.8g saturated fat, 0.24g sodium

Spicy Thai soup
The traditional tom yum soup uses the herbs and spices whole; I like to chop them finely so that you can eat all the soup. It really is the chicken soup of the East. So easy to make and the aroma is wonderful. Serves 4–6

1 garlic clove, crushed
2 tablespoons Thai fish sauce
3 small red chiles, including seeds included for spice
2–3 lemongrass stalks, finely chopped
1 inch cube fresh ginger root
1½ teaspoons Thai chili paste

6 fl oz vegetable broth, homemade (see page 138) or made with low-salt stock cubes
6 lime leaves (kaffir, dried, or fresh)
2 lbs boneless chicken, skinned and cut into strips
8 oz mixed mushrooms
Handful of fresh cilantro, chopped

Put the garlic, fish sauce, chiles, lemongrass, ginger, and chili paste in a blender and whizz to a smooth paste.
Put the broth in a saucepan and bring to a boil, then add the ingredients from the blender, together with the lime leaves, and simmer for 10 minutes.
Add the chicken and mushrooms and cook for another 20 minutes on a low heat.
When ready, serve garnished with chopped cilantro.

Per serving: 278 calories, 5.3g fat, 1.6g saturated fat, 0.81g sodium

Chicken soup
This dish is made all over the world. The Chinese make it for maintaining good strength and it has been known as "the Jewish penicillin" for centuries. It is very satisfying. **Serves 6**

1 tablespoon olive oil or vegetable (canola) oil
2 onions, diced
2 sticks celery, finely chopped
2 carrots, finely diced
1½ cup all-purpose flour

2 pints chicken broth, homemade (see page 139) or made with low-salt stock cubes
Freshly ground black pepper
1 lb boneless cooked chicken, skinned and chopped
1 tablespoon chopped parsley

Heat the oil in a large saucepan. Add the onions, celery, and carrots and cook for 3–4 minutes on a low heat.

Stir in the flour and cook for 1 minute, then add the chicken broth and bring to a boil. Season with black pepper and simmer for 10 minutes.

Add the cooked chicken and heat through for 5 minutes, then serve, garnished with parsley.

Per serving: 244 calories, 8g fat, 2.2g saturated fat, 0.17g sodium

Mixed herb salad
This salad is full of flavor, so you will not need much dressing to make it tasty. The best way to dress a salad is to put all of the salad ingredients in a large bowl, then add the dressing and toss well. **Serves 4**

1 Romaine lettuce
1 iceberg lettuce
12 cherry tomatoes, halved
½ cucumber, diced
Handful each of:
   fresh basil
   fresh cilantro
   fresh tarragon
   fresh parsley

For the dressing
6 tablespoons extra virgin olive oil
1 tablespoon Dijon mustard
Juice and shredded rind of 1 lemon
½ garlic clove, crushed

Cut up the lettuces and put in a bowl. Add the tomatoes and cucumber.

Now chop the herbs roughly and set aside.

In a different bowl, whisk together the olive oil, mustard, lemon juice and rind, and the garlic. Add the herbs, then use to dress the salad. Serve immediately.

Per serving: 196 calories, 17.9g fat, 2.4g saturated fat, 0.12g sodium

Bean salad *This has a wonderful Mediterranean feel to it and works equally well as a side dish or a lunch-time salad. It also makes a great partner to fish dishes.* **Serves 4**

5 oz can garbanzo beans
5 oz can red kidney beans
5 oz can lima beans
Juice and shredded rind of
   1 lemon

1 garlic clove, crushed
2 tablespoons extra virgin
   olive oil
Handful of fresh basil leaves
Freshly ground black pepper

Drain the beans and mix well in a large bowl.

Add the lemon juice and the garlic.

Add the olive oil and mix well.

Now shred the basil leaves and add to the bowl, together with the rind of the lemon. Season with black pepper and give another mix.

Refrigerate overnight for all the flavors to strengthen before you serve the salad.

Per serving: 119 calories, 6.4g fat, 0.8g saturated fat, 0.22g sodium

Four-mushroom salad with truffle oil
White truffle oil is an infused oil normally made with olive oil. The smell is fabulous and the oil is low in saturated fat. **Serves 4**

1½ lbs mushrooms (4 varieties —I like shiitake, portobello, oyster, and wild)
6 tablespoons olive oil
1 garlic clove, crushed

Freshly ground black pepper
8 oz arugula leaves
Juice of 1 lemon
4 tablespoons white truffle oil
Fresh basil leaves to serve

Cut the mushrooms into large wedges and cook in a large skillet with 3 tablespoons of the olive oil.

Add the garlic and cook on a medium heat for around 5 minutes.

Season with black pepper, then remove from the heat and set aside to cool.

In a mixing bowl, mix the arugula leaves, lemon juice, and remaining olive oil. Season with black pepper and mix well.

Add the mushrooms to the bowl and mix well again.

Divide between 4 serving plates, drizzle a tablespoon of white truffle oil over each one, garnish with fresh basil leaves, and serve.

Per serving: 295 calories, 28.3g fat, 3.2g saturated fat, 0.06g sodium

Arugula and tuna salad
Arugula has such a rich flavor and it is also very good for you in all the same ways as spinach. Serve with some fresh bread to mop up the delicious juices. **Serves 4**

4 fresh medium tuna steaks, around 1¼ inches thick
6 tablespoons olive oil
1 teaspoon English mustard
1 tablespoon white wine vinegar

3–3½ cups (5 oz) arugula leaves
8 sun-dried tomatoes, roughly chopped
Freshly ground black pepper

In a hot skillet, heat 1 tablespoon of the olive oil. Now sear 2 of the tuna steaks for 1 minute on each side. Cook the remaining 2 steaks in the same way and set them all aside. They will be rare, but this is the best way to eat fresh tuna.

In a bowl, whisk the remaining oil with the mustard and vinegar.

Put the arugula leaves and sun-dried tomatoes in a large mixing bowl, then add the dressing. Season with black pepper and mix again.

Divide the salad between 4 plates and top each with a tuna steak, cut in half at an angle and pointing upwards on the salad.

Per serving: 376 calories, 23.9g fat, 3.9g saturated fat, 0.16g sodium

Classic French salad

The French are so adventurous with their salads, using a huge variety of ingredients to make every bite different. Here is a classic French salad.

Serves 4

A little olive oil, for frying
6 bacon slices
1 egg
4 slices thick white bread, cut into ¼ inch cubes
4 Romaine lettuce heads
2 cups fresh spinach
Freshly ground black pepper

For the dressing
Juice of ½ lemon
1 teaspoon Dijon mustard
A few fresh basil leaves, torn
3 tablespoons extra virgin olive oil

Make the dressing by mixing the lemon juice, mustard, basil, and olive oil together well.

Now remove the fat from the bacon and cut the slices into ½ inch cubes.

In a hot skillet, heat a drizzle of oil and add the bacon. Cook on a medium heat until brown, then remove from the pan and set aside.

Poach the egg and set aside.

Add the cubed bread to the skillet you used to cook the bacon and fry for a few minutes with a little more oil until crispy.

Cut up the lettuce heads and place in a large mixing bowl with the spinach. Pour on the dressing and mix very well with your hands. Add the croûtons, bacon, poached egg, and black pepper and serve.

Per serving: 291 calories, 17.2g fat, 2.9g saturated fat, 0.72g sodium

Fresh tuna Niçoise

Using fresh tuna in this dish really makes a difference, although canned may be used as a substitute. This is a modern twist on the French classic and is a meal in itself. **Serves 4**

12 new potatoes
4 tablespoons olive oil
Freshly ground black pepper
2 garlic cloves, crushed, plus 1 small whole garlic clove
30 fine beans
8 quails' eggs

1 can pitted black olives (8 oz, drained)
3 tablespoons lemon juice
2 teaspoons Dijon mustard
1 tail end of fresh tuna (enough to be cut into 3 x 2 inch slices per person)

Preheat the oven to 375°F. Put the new potatoes in an ovenproof dish and add a little of the olive oil, plenty of black pepper and the crushed garlic. Mix well, then put in the oven and cook for 20–30 minutes, stirring occasionally.

Put the fine beans in a saucepan of boiling water and boil for 15 minutes. Drain, then run them immediately under cold water to keep their color. Set aside.

Put the quails' eggs in a saucepan of boiling water and boil for a few minutes. Drain, peel, and set aside.

Put the olives, half of the lemon juice, and the small garlic clove in a blender and whizz to a lumpy paste. (This can also be done with a hand-held blender.)

Put most of the remaining olive oil, the Dijon mustard, and the remaining lemon juice in a dish and mix to make a dressing. Set aside.

Heat a tiny amount of olive oil in a skillet (just enough to prevent sticking) and, when it is hot, add the tuna end in one piece. Fry on a high heat for about 15 seconds on each side and remove from the pan.

Slice the tuna into 2 inch wheels, putting 3 on each plate. Add the potatoes, followed by the beans.

Using spoons, make a quenelle of (what is now) the olive tapenade and add to the plates. Drizzle the dressing over the beans. Halve the quails' eggs, add to each salad and serve.

Per serving: 456 calories, 28.5g fat, 3.7g saturated fat, 0.47g sodium

Thai chicken salad
A very simple way to recreate all the flavors of Thailand without deep-frying the chicken. This dressing can be used for other salads too: it instantly adds zing!

Serves 4

4 chicken breasts, skinless
1 tablespoon vegetable (canola) oil
1 small bird's eye chile, finely chopped, not seeded
1 inch cube fresh ginger root, grated
2 lemongrass stalks, peeled and finely chopped
1 tablespoon chopped fresh mint
1 tablespoon brown sugar
1 garlic clove, crushed
Juice of 1 lemon
1 tablespoon reduced-salt soy sauce
1 tablespoon Thai fish sauce
4 cups fresh spinach
Lime wedges, to serve

Slice the chicken breasts into 1 inch pieces.
Heat the oil in a skillet and fry the chicken on a medium–high heat until it is cooked through. Try not to keep turning the chicken in the pan so that it gets a nice, caramelized glaze.
Meanwhile, put the chile, ginger, lemongrass, mint, sugar, lemon juice, garlic, soy sauce, and fish sauce in a bowl and mix together very well.
Add the cooked chicken to the bowl and mix again.
Now add the spinach (uncooked), mix well and serve as a salad at once, with lime wedges on the side.

Per serving: 206 calories, 4.6g fat, 0.7g saturated fat, 0.7g sodium

Chicken liver salad
Liver is rich in iron and chicken livers contain little fat. Do note, however, that women considering pregnancy or in the early stages of pregnancy should avoid liver. **Serves 4**

Salad leaves of your choice
4 cups spinach
1 tablespoon vegetable (canola) oil
1 small onion, finely chopped
1 lb chicken livers
1 teaspoon wholegrain mustard
2 tablespoons balsamic vinegar
Salt and freshly ground black pepper

Slice the salad leaves and put in a bowl with the spinach.
Heat the oil in a large skillet, add the onion and cook on a medium heat for 2 minutes.
Now sear the chicken livers in the same pan on a high heat, then reduce the heat and cook through: this should take 3–4 minutes. Add the mustard and the balsamic vinegar, remove from the heat and mix well.
Season and pour over the salad and serve on individual serving plates.

Per serving: 153 calories, 6g fat, 1.1g saturated fat, 0.26g sodium

3

Sides, Snacks, and Appetizers

Baked garlic

This is a must! Don't be wary of it, as when you cook garlic most of the pungency disappears. I love this on toasted ciabatta or other fresh, warm bread—just spread it on and enjoy it! **Serves 6**

1 garlic bulb
Olive oil
Few sprigs of fresh rosemary

Preheat the oven to 325°F.
Cut through the middle of the garlic bulb and drizzle with oil.
Stuff with the rosemary sprigs, push the two halves back together and wrap in foil.
Put in the oven and cook for 35 minutes.

Per serving: 16 calories, 0.9g fat, 0.1g saturated fat, 0g sodium

Roasted butternut squash and garlic

This is great as a snack or served with roasted chicken. Butternut squash has a wonderful, smooth texture and the best way to cook it is to keep it simple. **Serves 4–6**

4 medium butternut squash
4–6 tablespoons olive oil
Freshly ground black pepper
Pinch of cayenne pepper
1 garlic bulb

Preheat the oven to 425°F.
Peel the butternut squash using a potato peeler. Scoop out the seeds with a spoon and discard, then cut the flesh into 2 inch wedges. Put in a mixing bowl with 3 tablespoons of the olive oil and mix well. Season with black pepper and cayenne pepper and mix again, then transfer into an ovenproof dish.
Now break up the garlic bulb into single cloves. Do not peel. Add the cloves to the butternut and roast in the oven for 45 minutes. Add more oil if needed.

Per serving: 222 calories, 11.4g fat, 1.5g saturated fat, 0.01g sodium

Roast potatoes with sage

These potatoes work so well with the sage. They can be eaten as a snack or with a Sunday roast such as Italian-style Roast Chicken (see page 113) or Saffron Chicken (see page 114). **Serves 4**

6 baking potatoes
4 tablespoons olive oil or vegetable (canola) oil
Handful of fresh sage leaves, roughly chopped
Freshly ground black pepper

Preheat the oven to 425°F.
Peel the potatoes and quarter them. Place in a saucepan of boiling water for 5 minutes, drain and place on a baking sheet.
Add the oil and the sage leaves to the sheet. Mix all the ingredients together and season well with black pepper.
Place in the oven and cook for 50 minutes, turning them every 15 minutes to ensure even cooking.

Per serving: 327 calories, 11.7g fat, 1.6g saturated fat, 0.02g sodium

Low-fat chunky French fries

Very simple to make and so delicious you will forget that they are not deep-fried. Serve with any of the salad recipes or main dishes in this book. **Serves 4**

5 large baking potatoes
4 tablespoons olive oil or vegetable (canola) oil
Rock salt

Preheat the oven to 350°F.
Peel the potatoes and cut into large pieces around 1 inch thick.
Put the French fries in a large bowl and add the oil. Give them a good mix (using your hands works best).
Line a baking sheet with aluminum foil and lay the potato on it. Sprinkle with rock salt and cook in the oven for 30 minutes, giving them a good turn halfway through the cooking time so that they brown on all sides.

Per serving: 286 calories, 11.5g fat, 1.6g saturated fat, 0.21g sodium

Japanese-style beans

What a wonderful way to jazz up green beans! Make sure that you do not overcook the beans so that they stay nice and crunchy—you could cook them in a steamer if preferred. **Serves 4**

2 lbs fine beans	4 tablespoons sesame oil
1 tablespoon vegetable (canola) oil	2 tablespoons reduced-salt soy sauce
1 garlic clove, crushed	Dash of Tabasco sauce
4 tablespoons sesame seeds	Freshly ground black pepper

Put the beans in a saucepan of boiling water for 3 minutes. Drain.

Heat the oil in a large wok or skillet. Add the beans and garlic, fry for 1 minute on a medium–high heat, then add the remaining ingredients. Cook for a further minute and serve.

Per serving: 255 calories, 21.8g fat, 2.7g saturated fat, 0.33g sodium

Broccoli in oyster sauce

This works well with other Asian-style recipes in this book, such as Steamed Sea bass, Chinese Style (see page 110) or Chinese Wok-fried Pork (see page 114). **Serves 4**

2 lbs broccoli	3 tablespoons vegetable broth, homemade (see page 138) or made with low-salt stock cubes
1 tablespoon vegetable (canola) oil	
1 garlic clove, crushed	
2 tablespoons oyster sauce	1 tablespoon sesame oil
2 tablespoons reduced-salt soy sauce	

Put the broccoli in a saucepan of boiling water for 2 minutes, drain, and set aside. Heat the oil in a skillet and add the garlic. Cook for 1 minute on a medium heat then add the broccoli. **Add** the oyster sauce, soy sauce, and vegetable broth. Stir-fry for a further minute, drizzle the sesame soil on top and serve.

Per serving: 136 calories, 7.5g fat, 0.6g saturated fat, 0.66g sodium

Wok-fried tofu and spinach

If anyone says that tofu is boring, tell them to give this one a go. Great as a snack or you can add more vegetables for a complete dinner.

Serves 4

2 tablespoons vegetable (canola) oil

1½ lbs silken tofu (or any tofu), diced

3½–4 cups fresh spinach

1 garlic clove, crushed

Juice of 1 lime or lemon

4 tablespoons reduced-salt soy sauce

1 small bird's eye chile, finely chopped

1 inch cube fresh ginger root, shredded

1 lemongrass stalk, peeled and finely chopped

4 tablespoons water

Handful of fresh cilantro

Heat the oil in a wok or a large skillet.

Add the tofu pieces and fry on a medium heat for 1 minute, then turn and fry for a further minute. Add the spinach, turning the heat down to low. Add the garlic, lime or lemon juice, soy sauce, chile, ginger, and lemongrass and cook for 1 minute.

Add the water and cook for 1 more minute or so, turning all the time.

Serve garnished with fresh cilantro.

Per serving: 192 calories, 13.2g fat, 1.4g saturated fat, 0.71g sodium

Egg-fried rice

A great way to enjoy Chinese food without all the MSG! Kids will love this dish too. This is particularly good with Steamed Sea Bass, Chinese Style (see page 110) and Tiger Shrimp in Soy Sauce (see page 98). **Serves 4–6**

4 eggs

1 tablespoon vegetable (rapeseed) oil

1¼ lbs white rice, cooked

1 cup frozen green peas

3 tablespoons reduced-salt soy sauce

3 tablespoons sesame oil

6 scallions, finely chopped

Crack the eggs into a bowl and whisk for just a few seconds.

In a large skillet, heat the oil and cook the eggs as if you were scrambling them.

Add the rice to the pan and mix in well, keeping the heat on low to medium.

Add all the remaining ingredients, heat through thoroughly and serve.

Per serving: 392 calories, 17.4g fat, 3g saturated fat, 0.56g sodium

Avocado and tomato towers

A classic combination of flavors, presented in an unusual way. This is a terrific vegetarian option using great ingredients, but make sure they are ripe and fresh. **Serves 4**

6 large tomatoes
Freshly ground black pepper
1 small red chile, finely
    chopped
3 avocados
1 lemon

6 scallions
Handful of fresh basil
1 tablespoon balsamic vinegar
4 tablespoons extra virgin
    olive oil

Seed the tomatoes, chop them and season with pepper. Put in a bowl, add the chopped chile and set aside.

Chop the avocados into small cubes and squeeze the lemon all over them.

Chop the scallions and the basil finely and add to the avocados. Mix in well.

Place a pastry ring on a serving plate and half fill it with a quarter of the avocado mix. Then top with a quarter of the tomato mix. Lift off the ring and repeat on the remaining plates. Drizzle ¼ tablespoon of the balsamic vinegar, followed by 1 tablespoon of the olive oil, all around each of the 4 plates before serving.

Per serving: 315 calories, 29.9g fat, 3.8g saturated fat, 0.02g sodium

Bruschetta with tomato and basil

A wonderful canapé or appetizer—it is so fresh-tasting and always a winner at any dinner party. Feel free to experiment with your own topping ideas. **Serves 4–6**

I ciabatta loaf, sliced into
    1 inch slices
I large red onion, finely
    chopped
1 garlic clove, crushed
2 tablespoons olive oil

Juice of ½ lemon
1 small red chile, very finely
    chopped
Handful of fresh basil
8 medium tomatoes, seeded
    and chopped

Start by toasting the ciabatta, either under a broiler, in the oven or in a toaster.

In a large mixing bowl mix the onion, garlic, olive oil, lemon juice, and chile. Now take the basil leaves, roll them up together, almost like a cigar, and slice. Add these to the bowl, then add the chopped tomatoes.

To serve, top each ciabatta slice with some of the mix.

Per serving: 297 calories, 9g fat, 0.8g saturated fat, 0.42g sodium

Variation

Bruschetta with pea tapenade *This is a nice alternative to the traditional bruschetta topping. It can also be made just as a dip.*

Place 7 ounces cooked green peas, 1 crushed garlic clove, 6 tablespoons fromage frais, and 2 tablespoons olive oil in a blender and whizz until smooth. Spread on the ciabatta and serve.

Per serving: 321 calories, 11g fat, 2.1g saturated fat, 0.6g sodium

Eggplant and feta stacks

This is a very impressive-looking dish—like a creation from a top-class restaurant. It is very simple to make and is always a hit at a dinner party. **Serves 4**

2 medium eggplant
3 tablespoons olive oil
10 large tomatoes, seeded and
   finely chopped
Handful of fresh basil leaves,
   shredded
1 clove garlic, crushed
5 oz feta cheese, crumbled
Freshly ground black pepper
4 tablespoons pine nuts

For the sauce
11 oz canned tomatoes
1 small red chile
1 tablespoon extra virgin
   olive oil

Preheat the oven to 350°F.

Slice the eggplant into circles 1 inch thick and fry in 2 tablespoons oil in a non-stick skillet for about 3–4 minutes on each side. Set aside when they are all cooked.

Place the tomatoes in a large mixing bowl together with the basil, garlic, and cheese. Now add the remaining oil followed by some black pepper and mix well.

In a non-stick skillet with no oil, fry the pine nuts for 1 minute, tossing them continuously so that they do not burn. Add them to the tomato mixture and combine all the ingredients together.

Place 4 of the largest eggplant rounds on a baking sheet and drop some of the tomato mixture on to each one. Choose the next biggest rounds of eggplant and place on the top, followed by more tomato mixture, alternating until you have 4 neat pyramid-like stacks.

Place in the oven and cook for 10–12 minutes until heated through.

Meanwhile, to make the sauce, whizz the tomatoes in a blender with the chile and olive oil until smooth.

Divide the tomato sauce between 4 serving plates, then top with an eggplant stack and serve.

Per serving: 353 calories, 27.1g fat, 7.1g saturated fat, 0.6g sodium

Asparagus raft with salmon roe on avocado broth

Avocado is a perfect way to include the right fats in your diet. It is also delicious and this dish is very light and tasty. **Serves 4**

24–30 medium asparagus
   spears
1 ripe avocado
½ cup vegetable broth,
   homemade (see page 138)
   or made with low-salt
   stock cubes, cooled

Freshly ground black pepper
2½ oz salmon roe
Herb oil, to garnish

You will need to make the asparagus equal-sized. Taking around 4 at a time and starting at the tips, cut off around 3 inches. Using one of these tips as a measure, take the same amount off the remaining stalks. Discard the uneven leftovers.

Add the asparagus to a saucepan of boiling water. Cook for 3 minutes, then run under ice-cold water. This stops the cooking process and keeps the asparagus green and crunchy.

Now, in a blender, whizz the avocado and the broth and season well with black pepper.

To serve, put a few spoonfuls of this mix in the base of each plate. Next, make a raft with your asparagus on two levels— the first lined up one way, then the next level going the other way. Top with some salmon roe.

Drizzle some herb oil around the edge of the avocado broth to garnish.

Per serving: 121 calories, 9.9g fat, 1.1g saturated fat, 0.23g sodium

Marinated salmon sashimi

This dish is for the nervous sushi eater—the salmon is marinated in lemon juice that cures the fish, killing any bacteria in the same way that cooking does. **Serves 4**

1½ lbs fresh skinless boneless salmon

1 medium red onion

Juice of 2 lemons

4 tablespoons reduced-salt soy sauce

1 teaspoon wasabi paste

Cut the salmon into small cubes and set aside in a mixing bowl.

Now chop the red onion very, very finely and add to the salmon.

Pour the lemon juice all over the salmon and onion and let it stand for 5 minutes.

In a separate bowl, mix together the soy sauce and the wasabi paste. Add to the salmon and mix well. Refrigerate for at least 30 minutes before serving.

A great way to serve this is in a Martini glass.

Per serving: 337 calories, 19.4g fat, 3.9g saturated fat, 0.73g sodium

Salmon and dill mousse

Salmon is rich in omega-3 oils and low in saturated fat. Don't let the mousse put you off—this dish is quick, easy, and foolproof! Serve on salad leaves or with melba or rye toast. **Serves 4**

1 lb skinless boneless salmon

2 tablespoons plain low-fat yogurt

½ small red chile (seeded for a less spicy flavor)

Juice of ½ lemon

1 egg

2 tablespoons fresh dill

Put all the ingredients in a blender and blend until smooth.

Divide the mix between 4 ramekin dishes.

Now take a large skillet and add water to it, around 1–2 inches deep. Put the ramekins in the pan, cover and cook on a low to medium heat for 8–12 minutes or until the mousse is firm.

Slip a knife around the edge of each ramekin and the mousse should slide out.

Serve cold.

Per serving: 226 calories, 13.9g fat, 2.9g saturated fat, 0.07g sodium

Baked sardines

Sardines are an underrated fish. They are full of all the right oils and so delicious. Drink a glass of rosé wine with this and enjoy—you will think you are in the Mediterranean! **Serves 4**

4 lemons
12 fresh large sardines, gutted
2 tablespoons olive oil
2 garlic cloves, crushed
4 tablespoons chopped fresh oregano
Freshly ground black pepper

Preheat the oven to 375°F.

Grate the rind from 2 of the lemons and set aside in a small bowl. Squeeze the juice from the rindless lemons.

Put the sardines in an ovenproof dish.

In a bowl, mix the olive oil, lemon juice, garlic, and oregano. Drizzle this mixture over the fish and season with black pepper.

Put in the oven for 25–30 minutes.

Cut the remaining lemons into wedges. Serve the sardines hot, sprinkled with lemon rind and accompanied by the lemon wedges.

Per serving: 396 calories, 23.8g fat, 4.4g saturated fat, 0.24g sodium

Tuna tartare
Make sure that you ask for fresh tuna at the fish counter and say that you will be using it sushi-style. Alternatively, marinate in lemon juice for 20 minutes to cure the fish and kill bacteria (in the same way cooking does). **Serves 4**

14 oz fresh tuna, finely sliced
2 tablespoons chopped
  scallions
2 tablespoons sesame seeds
2 tablespoons reduced-salt
  soy sauce

Juice of 2 limes
2 tablespoons sesame oil
Handful of fresh cilantro,
  chopped
Herb oil, to serve

When slicing the tuna, discard any parts that have a grain as you really want only the flesh you can cut through with ease. In a bowl, combine the tuna, scallions, sesame seeds, soy sauce, lime juice, and sesame oil. Mix well, then add the cilantro.
To serve restaurant-style, take a steel pastry ring around 3 inches in diameter and place on a serving plate. Fill with the mixture, press down hard and then remove the ring. Drizzle with herb oil. Repeat with the rest of the mixture and serve.

Per serving: 255 calories, 16.6g fat, 2.7g saturated fat, 0.37g sodium

Mediterranean marinated tuna
The tuna in this dish is served raw. If you have any reservations about this you can marinate it in lemon juice for 15 minutes—it will cure the fish and kill any bacteria. **Serves 4**

14 oz fresh tuna, cubed
2 tablespoons sun-dried
  tomato paste
½ garlic clove, crushed
4 scallions, finely chopped
2 tablespoons pitted black
  olives, chopped

2 tablespoons olive oil or
  vegetable (canola) oil
Handful of fresh basil leaves,
  shredded
1 tablespoon pine nuts
Juice of I lemon

Put the tuna pieces in a large mixing bowl and add the sun-dried tomato paste, garlic, scallions, olives, oil, basil, and pine nuts. Mix well.
Add the lemon juice just before serving and stir in well.
Press the mixture into metal pastry rings to give it a good shape for serving.

Per serving: 240 calories, 15.3g fat, 2.1g saturated fat, 0.12g sodium

Chicken with a honey glaze

This has a superb barbecue taste only without the hassle of having to cook outside. It's a dish that is popular with children. Serve with a salad or baked potato. **Serves 4**

3 tablespoons honey

3 tablespoons tomato paste

1 garlic clove, crushed

1 teaspoon white wine vinegar

2 sprigs fresh thyme

1 tablespoon Dijon mustard

4 large chicken fillets, skinless

Preheat the oven to 400°F.

Mix all the ingredients together apart from the chicken.

Place the chicken breasts on a baking sheet and top each one generously with the sauce. Bake in the for 25 minutes and serve.

Per serving: 206 calories, 2g fat, 0.5g saturated fat, 0.25g sodium

Oriental chicken wraps

This dish works equally well with chicken or pork and looks stunning presented in the radicchio leaves. Smaller wraps make great canapés. Serve with warm pita bread. **Serves 4**

1 tablespoon vegetable (canola) oil

1 small onion, finely chopped

10 large mushrooms, finely chopped

1 lb lean ground chicken

1 garlic clove, crushed

1 tablespoon sesame seeds

1 tablespoon sesame oil

3 oz canned water chestnuts, chopped

1 tablespoon reduced-salt soy sauce

1 tablespoon oyster sauce

1 radicchio

Add the oil to a large heated skillet and cook the onion and mushrooms for 2–3 minutes.

Add the chicken and garlic and cook for 5–8 minutes, stirring continuously. Once the chicken is cooked add the sesame seeds, sesame oil, water chestnuts, soy sauce, and oyster sauce. Stir and cook for a further minute so that the ingredients caramelize and all the flavors blend.

Remove several leaves from the radicchio and fill each one with some of the chicken mix.

Serve hot.

Per serving: 218 calories, 10g fat, 1.7g saturated fat, 0.41g sodium

Classic American burger

The best-tasting burger is always made using the finest, leanest beef. This really has to be tried—burgers are rarely made like this any more. Try serving with tomato salsa (see page 135). **Serves 4**

1 slice brown bread
2 lbs lean ground Angus beef
1 garlic clove, crushed
1 teaspoon finely chopped
   fresh thyme
1 tablespoon tomato paste
1 tablespoon Dijon mustard

1 egg
Freshly ground black pepper
Dash of Tabasco sauce
Splash of vegetable (canola)
   oil, for frying
Toasted sesame-seed burger
   buns, to serve

Whizz the bread in a blender to make crumbs.

Place all the remaining ingredients (except for the oil and the buns) in a large mixing bowl and, adding the breadcrumbs, mix with your hands so it all comes together. Make into patties.

Heat a little oil in a skillet and cook the patties for 2–3 minutes on each side; keep on the medium-rare side.

Serve on toasted sesame-seed buns.

Per serving: 643 calories, 31.8g fat, 11.7g saturated fat, 0.68g sodium

Tandoori spiced lamb
This recipe works equally well with chicken or pork. It has great Indian flavors without all the oil. You could cook this on a barbecue outside, if the weather permits! **Serves 4**

4 large lean lamb steaks
(about 12 oz in total)
1 lemon, quartered
For the marinade
2 garlic cloves, crushed
1 small onion, quartered
1 inch cube fresh ginger root, grated
2 teaspoons ground cumin
2 teaspoons ground coriander
1 teaspoon garam masala
½ teaspoon cayenne pepper
2 tablespoons lime juice
4 tablespoons plain low-fat yogurt

Put all the ingredients for the marinade in a food-processor and whizz until smooth. Remove any fat from the lamb steaks, then coat them with the marinade. You can keep them marinating in the fridge for a day to develop a more intense flavor, if you have time.

When you are ready to cook the lamb, preheat the oven to 400°F.

Put the lamb on a baking sheet and cook in the oven for 30 minutes turning twice.

Serve each steak with a wedge of lemon.

Per serving: 178 calories, 8.2g fat, 3.5g saturated fat, 0.08g sodium

Liver and onion on toast
Liver is high in iron and very low in fat. But do note that women considering pregnancy or in the early stages of pregnancy should avoid liver. I love this spread as a starter on toasted triangles. **Serves 4**

8 eggs
3 tablespoons vegetable (canola) oil
1 large onion, chopped
1 lb chicken livers
Salt and freshly ground black pepper
Toasted triangles or crackers, to serve

Start by hard-cooking the eggs (in a saucepan of boiling water for 5 minutes). Cool, peel and set aside.

Heat 2 tablespoons of the oil in a skillet, then add the onion. Cook for around 4 minutes until slightly caramelized.

Add the chicken livers and cook with the remaining oil for about 4 minutes, ensuring that they remain tender on the inside and are not overcooked.

Put the mixture in a food-processor, together with the eggs, and season well. Blend but do not purée—keep it a little chunky.

Serve with toast or crackers.

Per serving: 419 calories, 22.7g fat, 4.5g saturated fat, 0.48g sodium

4

Penne with sun-dried tomatoes and pine nuts

The way to get the best results with any pasta dish is to add the cooked pasta to the pan of sauce so that it is well coated. **Serves 4–6**

4 cups penne
3–4 oz sun-dried tomatoes in
  oil, drained
1 small red bird's eye chile
3 tablespoons olive oil

4 oz pine nuts
1 garlic clove, crushed
Freshly ground black pepper
Handful of fresh basil leaves,
  torn

Boil the pasta according to the instructions on the packet.

In a blender, whizz the sun-dried tomatoes and chile until smooth. Add some olive oil if needed but not the oil from the tomatoes as it is too strong.

Heat a large skillet and add the pine nuts—toast them without oil, just in the dry pan. This happens quickly, so keep an eye on them and set aside when done.

Now add 1 tablespoon of olive oil to the pan and fry the garlic for 30 seconds. Add the sun-dried tomatoes and remaining olive oil and cook on a low heat for a further minute.

Add the penne and pine nuts. Stir in well, season with black pepper, and serve with some torn basil leaves.

Per serving: 723 calories, 34.4g fat, 4.2g saturated fat, 0.39g sodium

White truffle and mushroom risotto

It is not only olive oil that is low in saturated fat—try infused oils such as white truffle or sesame oil. They have more flavor and less is required to flavor your cooking. **Serves 4**

1 large onion
2 large carrots
6 shiitake mushrooms
6 tablespoons truffle oil
2 garlic cloves, crushed
11 oz risotto rice
1 glass of white wine
  (optional)

4 cups vegetable broth,
  homemade (see page 138)
  or made with low-salt
  stock cubes
10–14 button mushrooms
2 tablespoons truffle oil and a
  handful of finely chopped
  parsley, to serve

Chop the onion and carrots finely and cut the mushrooms into thin slices. Set aside.

In a large saucepan, heat 3 tablespoons of the truffle oil. Add the onion and cook for 2–3 minutes. Add the carrots and garlic and stir for 1 minute. Add the mushrooms and cook for a further minute.

Now add the risotto rice and coat with the mix in the pan. Add the wine, if using, and allow to simmer for a minute.

Meanwhile, have your broth in a separate saucepan on a boil. Add it to the rice mixture a ladle at a time and keep stirring for 20 minutes. When you are almost done add the remaining truffle oil.

Divide the risotto between 4 plates, then drizzle some truffle oil around each plate and sprinkle with parsley.

Per serving: 5038 calories, 23.3g fat, 3.3g saturated fat, 0.15g sodium

Spaghetti with caramelized vegetables

This can be done with a variety of vegetables, so just use the list below as a guide. Normally Parmesan cheese is added to pasta but you hardly need it in this dish. **Serves 4**

4 cups spaghetti
4 tablespoons olive oil or vegetable (canola) oil
1 onion, finely chopped
12 button mushrooms, sliced
12 asparagus spears, cut into ½ inch pieces
2 zucchini, diced
1 garlic clove, crushed
1 tablespoon balsamic vinegar
3–4 oz sun-dried tomatoes in oil, drained and diced
1 tablespoon tomato paste
Freshly ground black pepper
Handful of fresh basil leaves
Parmesan cheese, shredded, to serve (optional)

Cook the spaghetti according to the instructions on the packet. Drain and set aside.

In a large saucepan, heat half the oil on a high heat, then add the onion and cook for 4 minutes.

Turn the heat to medium and add the mushrooms, asparagus, zucchini, and garlic. Add the remaining oil and the vinegar and cook for 5 minutes until all the vegetables are caramelized.

Add the tomatoes and tomato paste and stir in well, then add the spaghetti to the pan and coat thoroughly.

Season and add the basil, tearing it as you do so. Serve with a little Parmesan if you wish.

Per serving (withour Parmesan): 570 calories, 17.2g fat, 2.4g saturated fat, 0.4g sodium

Gnocchi with wild mushroom sauce

Gnocchi are easy to cook. All you do is add them to boiling water and as soon as they float to the top they are ready. Keep it simple to enjoy the texture. **Serves 4–6**

1 lb gnocchi
4 tablespoons olive oil
1 garlic clove, crushed
1½ lbs mixed mushrooms, sliced
1½ tablespoons white wine
1 tablespoon white truffle oil (optional)
Chopped fresh chives, to garnish

In a large saucepan of boiling water, cook the gnocchi until they float to the top (this should take around 3 minutes). Drain and set aside.

In another large saucepan, heat half the olive oil and cook the garlic for 30 seconds. Add the white wine, stir for a few seconds and then add the mushrooms and cook over a medium heat, stirring continuously, for 5 minutes. Add the remaining olive oil and cook for a further 2–3 minutes. Transfer to a blender and blend to a rough texture, not a purée.

Return the mixture to the pan along with the gnocchi and just heat through, coating the gnocchi well.

To serve, drizzle with white truffle oil, if using, and sprinkle with chopped chives.

Per serving: 297 calories, 12g fat, 1.8g saturated fat, 0.5g sodium

Tiger shrimp in soy sauce

This dish is really easy to make. Shrimp have no fat and should be cooked just until they turn pink—never overcook them. Serve with Egg-fried Rice (see page 79). **Serves 4**

25–30 large raw tiger shrimp, with heads and shells on
1 tablespoon vegetable (canola) oil
5 tablespoons dry white wine
3 garlic cloves, crushed
Juice of 2 large lemons
2 tablespoons reduced-salt soy sauce
6 scallions, chopped

Start by deveining the shrimp. To do this, cut down the center of each shrimp with a knife. If there is a dark vein there, take it out. (This also helps the shrimp to absorb all the flavor of the sauce.)

In a large wok (non-stick is best), heat the oil and then add the shrimp. Cook for 2 minutes on a high heat, turning frequently.

Add the wine and let the alcohol burn off for another minute. The shrimp should now be changing color, from gray to pink.

Add the garlic and cook for 1 more minute, then add the lemon juice and soy sauce. Toss the shrimp around and cook until they are completely pink.

Serve garnished with the chopped scallions.

Per serving: 122 calories, 3.5g fat, 0.3g saturated fat, 0.85g sodium

Mixed bean chili

A great vegetarian alternative to the traditional meat chili recipe. Try experimenting with different combinations of beans. The fresh ginger in my recipe adds heat, but you could add chiles as well if you like. **Serves 4**

1 tablespoon olive oil or vegetable (canola) oil
1 onion, finely chopped
2 garlic cloves, crushed
1 green bell pepper, seeded and finely chopped
1 red bell pepper, seeded and finely chopped
1 inch cube fresh ginger root, shredded
3 tablespoons tomato paste
14 oz can chopped tomatoes
14 oz can kidney beans, drained
14 oz can lima beans, drained
14 oz can garbanzo beans, drained
Fresh parsley or cilantro, to serve

In a large saucepan, heat the oil and add the onion. Cook for a few minutes, then add the garlic. Add the peppers and cook for a few more minutes, adding a little more oil if needed.

Add the ginger, tomato paste, and tomatoes. Mix in well for 1 minute before adding all the beans. Simmer for a few minutes so everything is warm.

Serve sprinkled with parsley or cilantro.

Per serving: 257 calories, 5.6g fat, 0.4g saturated fat, 0.72g sodium

Salmon fishcakes

These fishcakes are just bursting with flavor. Unlike many other fishcakes these are not deep-fried, making them light and so very fresh. You can adjust the chile content to your liking. **Serves 4**

4 fresh salmon fillets (about 1 lb in total)
1 red chile (seeded if you like it less spicy), roughly chopped
Juice of 1 lime or ½ lemon
1 egg (or enough to bind)
1 inch cube fresh ginger root, shredded
1 teaspoon Thai fish sauce (optional)
1 teaspoon reduced-salt soy sauce
2 lemongrass stalks
4 scallions, sliced
Handful of fresh cilantro leaves, chopped
2 tablespoons vegetable (canola) oil

Whizz the salmon, red chile, lime or lemon juice, egg, ginger, fish sauce (if using), and soy sauce in a blender to a rough consistency.

Peel the lemongrass stalks until you get to the tender root (the point at which you are able to slice through it with ease). Chop roughly and add to the blender. Whizz again for 1 minute.

Stir the scallions and cilantro into the mix.

Mold the salmon mixture into small balls and flatten slightly. Heat a large skillet and add a drizzle of vegetable oil.

Fry the fishcakes, 3 at a time, cooking for 2–3 minutes on each side. Be careful not to move them around the pan until they are ready or they will crumble as there is little fat in the mixture and no bread to bind it. Add a drizzle more oil to the pan as needed.

Serve warm.

Per serving: 277 calories, 19.3g fat, 3.2g saturated fat, 0.12g sodium

Poached salmon with five herbs

Another simple dish that makes the most of the flavors of fresh herbs. This recipe works equally well with white fish such as cod or haddock. **Serves 4**

4 x 4 oz salmon fillets, skinless
Handful each fresh:
basil
parsley
tarragon
chives
cilantro
Freshly ground black pepper

Put the salmon fillets in a large saucepan. Add just enough water to cover the fish and bring to a boil. As soon as it boils remove from the heat, cover the pan with a lid, and set aside for 15 minutes.

Put all the herbs together and chop until fine. A mezzaluna is perfect for doing this.

Now carefully lift the salmon fillets out of the water and set aside to cool to room temperature, before coating with the herbs on each side. Season with black pepper and serve at room temperature or chilled, with a salad.

Per serving: 208 calories, 12.5g fat, 2.5g saturated fat, 0.05g sodium

Cod baked in couscous and sun-dried tomato paste

If you can't find sun-dried tomato paste, just blend some sun-dried tomatoes with a little olive oil, lemon juice, garlic, and basil until smooth. **Serves 4**

7 oz couscous
1 egg
4 fillets cod, skinless

4 tablespoons sun-dried tomato paste
1 lemon
Fresh basil, to serve

Preheat the oven to 350°F.

Place the couscous in a bowl. Cover with boiling water and then put a plate on the top. Set aside for 5 minutes. When the couscous is ready, fluff it up with a fork.

Crack the egg into a bowl and whisk for just a few seconds.

Now take each cod fillet and dip it in the egg, then coat it with the couscous on all sides. Press down hard to make a crust.

Set all the coated fillets on a baking sheet and spread a tablespoon of sun-dried tomato paste on each one using a knife. Place in the oven and bake for 17–20 minutes.

Serve with fresh basil and a salad or mashed potatoes.

Per serving: 295 calories, 7.8g fat, 0.7g saturated fat, 0.17g sodium

Mediterranean-style baked cod

The sun-dried tomato mixture is so easy to make and will last in the refrigerator for many weeks. Use it for other fish and seafood, on bruschetta as a canapé, or with vegetables as a dip. **Serves 4**

4 x 6 oz cod fillets (with or without the skin)
Freshly ground black pepper
6 plum tomatoes, seeded
1 garlic clove
Juice of 1 lemon

½ small red chile, seeded if preferred
1 tablespoon olive oil
Handful of fresh basil leaves
9 oz can sun-dried tomatoes in olive oil, drained

Preheat the oven to 350°F.

Put the cod fillets on a baking sheet and season with black pepper.

In a blender, whizz the plum tomatoes, garlic, lemon juice, chile, olive oil, basil, and sun-dried tomatoes until roughly blended.

Spoon some tomato paste onto each cod fillet and bake in the oven for 18 minutes. Serve.

Per serving: 264 calories, 10g fat, 1.3g saturated fat, 0.71g sodium

Whole sea bass Niçoise

All the elements of the Salade Niçoise are here but in this version they are baked in the oven together, and the fish is left whole, giving you maximum flavor. **Serves 4**

6 new potatoes, quartered
30 fine beans
5 tablespoons olive oil
5 tablespoons lemon juice
4 whole sea bass, descaled
14–18 pitted black olives
6 anchovy fillets in oil, drained
Freshly ground black pepper
Handful of fresh parsley,
   roughly chopped, to garnish

Preheat the oven to 425°F.

Blanch the potatoes and beans in boiling water for 5 minutes, then drain and set aside.

In a large, deep baking dish, mix together the oil and lemon juice, then put the fish in the dish, side by side.

Put the potatoes on the fish, then scatter the beans, olives, and anchovies all over the top. Season with black pepper and bake in the oven for 40 minutes.

Garnish with fresh parsley and serve with bread—wonderful to mop up all the sauce.

Per serving: 418 calories, 24.9g fat, 3.6g saturated fat, 0.54g sodium

Baked mackerel parcels

You can also cook this on a barbecue, that will make it taste even better. Any white fish can be cooked like this and you can use whatever fresh herbs you have to hand. **Serves 2**

2 whole mackerel, gutted and
   cleaned
Freshly ground black pepper
1 lemon
4 fresh rosemary sprigs
2 garlic cloves, sliced
1 small red onion, thinly sliced
4 tablespoons white wine
Handful of fresh parsley,
   chopped

Preheat the oven to 400°F.

Put each fish on a large piece of aluminum foil on a baking sheet and season inside and out with black pepper.

Slice the lemon, then cut each slice in half. Place the lemon slices inside each fish with a couple of rosemary sprigs and a few garlic slices. Scatter the onion on top and pour the wine over each fish.

Wrap the foil loosely around each fish to make a parcel, and bake in the oven for 25 minutes.

Sprinkle over the chopped parsley to serve.

Per serving: 376 calories, 24.5g fat, 4.9g saturated fat, 0.1g sodium

Sea bass baked in Asian parcels

This is light but with a powerful flavor. It fills the room with an incredible aroma. Icefish, red snapper, or halibut are also suitable for this method of cooking. **Serves 4**

2 leeks
4 thick fillets of sea-bass
4 scallions
4 lemongrass stalks
12 new potatoes, cut in half
  and parboiled for 5 minutes
4 large mushrooms, cut in half

1 small red chile, seeded and
  finely chopped
1 large carrot, finely shredded
¾ cup dry white wine
2 tablespoons coconut milk
Juice of 1 lemon
Freshly ground black pepper

Preheat the oven to 325°F.

Take 4 x 12 inch squares of aluminum foil and make each one into the shape of a large bowl. Now double each one up with a second sheet of foil.

Slice the leeks into small strings and divide between the 4 foil parcels, placing them in the bottom of each one.

Add a whole scallion to each parcel, followed by a lemongrass stalk that should be cut in half. Now add 6 potato halves, 2 mushroom halves, and a little of the chopped chile to each parcel. Place some shredded carrot in each one, then place the fish fillets on the top. (Cooked in this way, the fish will steam rather than poach.)

In a bowl, mix the white wine, coconut milk, and lemon juice and season with black pepper. Pour over the sea bass in the 4 parcels.

Take 4 more large squares of foil and cover each parcel, making it dome-like and folding the joins well so that they are airtight. Now cook in the oven for 40 minutes.

When they are ready, place each parcel on a plate and take to the table. Then, using a large knife, make an incision from top to bottom.

This dish is eaten in the foil, that keeps all the flavors and aromas right in front of you as you eat.

Per serving: 336 calories, 7.2g fat, 2g saturated fat, 0.17g sodium

Seared tuna steak and asparagus

The key to cooking fresh tuna is to pan-fry it, searing it on a high heat. This locks in the juices without drying out the fish. Tuna is always better slightly undercooked. **Serves 4**

2 tablespoons vegetable
  (canola) oil or olive oil
4 large tuna steaks
2 lbs asparagus spears
1½ tablespoons dry white wine

Juice and shredded rind of
  1 lemon
Handful of fresh parsley,
  roughly chopped
Freshly ground black pepper

Run the oil over both sides of the tuna steaks. You oil the fish in this recipe, not the pan—it is a great way to cut down on oil without the food sticking.

Break the ends off the asparagus (they will break off at different points, but this is the natural way to remove the hard, inedible parts). Put the trimmed asparagus in a saucepan of boiling water and cook for 2–3 minutes, then rinse immediately under cold water, drain and set aside.

In a non-stick skillet on a high heat, sear the tuna steaks for just 1 minute on each side. Remove from the pan and set aside.

Using the same pan, fry the asparagus on a medium–high heat for 3–4 minutes. Add the wine to deglaze the pan, then add the lemon juice, rind, and black pepper to taste and cook for 1 minute.

Transfer the asparagus to a serving plate, top with the tuna steaks, pour the pan juices over the top, and garnish with parsley.

Per serving: 369 calories, 15.8g fat, 2.7g saturated fat, 0.1g sodium

Red snapper with orange, lemon, and lime

If you have ever been to the Caribbean or the Florida Keys, this will remind you of your visit; it is just so fresh in taste. **Serves 4**

Shredded rind of 1 orange and 6 tablespoons fresh orange juice

Shredded rind and juice of 1 lemon

Juice of 1 lime

5 tablespoons white wine

1 garlic clove, crushed

1 inch cube fresh ginger root, shredded

Freshly ground black pepper

4 fillets red snapper

Lemon or orange wedges to serve

Preheat the oven to 350°F.

Mix together all of the ingredients apart from the fish and the citrus fruit wedges.

Make 3 cuts on each side of each fish fillet. Now place the fillets in the mixture and refrigerate for at least 30 minutes.

Transfer the fish, together with the sauce, to an ovenproof dish.

Bake in the oven for 18–20 minutes and serve with lemon or orange wedges.

Per serving: 187 calories, 2.4g fat, 0.4g saturated fat, 0.14g sodium

Fish risotto
Any fish will work with this recipe. Sometimes your fish merchant or fresh fish counter may have leftover trimmings—you can get a great mix at incredible value this way. **Serves 4–6**

3–4 tablespoons olive oil
1 large onion, finely chopped
2 garlic cloves, crushed
1½ cups risotto rice
⅓–½ cup white wine

4 cups fish broth, homemade (see page 139) or made with low-salt stock cubes
5 oz cod, cubed
5 oz salmon, cubed
5 oz red snapper, cubed
Fresh parsley, to garnish

Heat 3 tablespoons of the olive oil in a large saucepan. Add the onion and cook on a high heat for 2–3 minutes. Add the garlic and stir for 1 minute.

Add the rice and coat with the oil in the pan for 1–2 minutes, then add the wine and simmer for a further minute.

Have your broth ready in a separate saucepan on a boil. Add it a ladle at a time to the rice mixture, stirring continuously for 20 minutes.

Just 5 minutes before the rice is ready add all the fish and cook through. This takes very little time.

Serve the risotto topped with parsley. I like to use a pastry ring as a mold to make the risotto into a nice, round shape.

Per serving: 546 calories, 14.4g fat, 2.3g saturated fat, 0.22g sodium

Soupe de poisson
This is a classic French dish. The French often serve it with a rouille—*a mayonnaise—but I feel there is so much flavor that this is not needed. Serve with crusty French bread.* **Serves 4–6**

3 tablespoons olive oil
1 onion, finely chopped
4 garlic cloves, crushed
3 lbs trimmings from 4 medium fish, such as red snapper, salmon, sea bass (a mix is great)
3–4 tablespoons tomato paste (4 for a richer taste)

Handful of fresh parsley, chopped
1 bay leaf
Sprig of fresh thyme
Salt and freshly ground black pepper
2 small red chiles, very finely diced
1 tablespoon paprika
4 cups water

In a large saucepan, heat the olive oil and fry the onion for 2 minutes.

Add the garlic and cook for a further minute.

Add all the remaining ingredients to the pan and cook for 1 hour on a low heat. Discard the bay leaf and sprig of thyme before serving.

Per serving: 478 calories, 21.5g fat, 3.7g saturated fat, 0.38g sodium

Fresh fish burger on ciabatta

If you use fresh fish and broil it, it's as good as any deep-fried fish that I have ever had. The capers and Dijon mustard give this a real kick. **Serves 4**

1 tablespoon capers
2 tablespoons light
   mayonnaise
1 tablespoon Dijon mustard

4 fillets swordfish or halibut,
   skinless
2 tablespoons olive oil
Shredded rind of 1 lemon
4 ciabatta buns, toasted

Preheat the broiler.

Roughly chop the capers and place in a mixing bowl with the mayonnaise and the mustard. Mix well and set aside.

Place the fish fillets on a baking sheet, brush with the olive oil and the lemon rind and broil for 3 minutes on each side.

Top the ciabatta with the mayonnaise mix, then the fish and serve with fresh salad leaves.

Per serving: 387 calories, 16.9g fat, 2.7g saturated fat, 0.8g sodium

Steamed sea bass, Chinese style

This dish is wonderful in its simplicity—try it with any whole fish. I recommend investing in a steamer: it's such an easy and healthy way to cook fish and vegetables. **Serves 4**

4 whole sea bass (or any
   whole fish)
4 scallions, each sliced into
   3–4 pieces
2 tablespoons reduced-salt
   soy sauce

1 inch cube fresh ginger root,
   shredded
2 tablespoons sesame oil
2 tablespoons vegetable
   (canola) oil

You can either get your fish merchant to remove the scales and gut the fish or you can do it yourself—it is very easy. Just use the back of a knife and scrape up and down the fish. All the scales come off this way. Then slice through the belly and remove everything under cold water to gut the fish.

Place the fish in a large steamer (bamboo is best). Top the fish with the scallions, soy sauce, ginger, and sesame oil and steam on a medium heat for 18–22 minutes.

In a small pan, heat the vegetable oil. Pour the hot oil over the fish to make a crackle on the skin.

Serve with rice.

Per serving: 305 calories, 16g fat, 2.1g saturated fat, 0.46g sodium

Sticky lemon chicken
Taking the skin off the chicken will dramatically reduce the amount of saturated fat without losing the flavor. Serve on a bed of arugula leaves for color and taste and/or with rice. **Serves 4**

8 chicken portions (breasts and legs or thighs)
3 lemons
2 tablespoons runny honey
3 garlic cloves, unpeeled
1 tablespoon olive oil
2–3 sprigs of fresh rosemary

Preheat the oven to 350°F.
Squeeze the juice from the lemons into a large baking dish. Now add the honey, garlic cloves, and olive oil and mix well. Add the chicken pieces to the dish and put the empty lemon halves all around it. (It is surprising how much more juice will be released from the used lemons during the cooking time.)
Put the sprigs of rosemary in the dish and bake for 1 hour. The lemons will come out all sticky and caramelized and can be eaten too.

Per serving: 344 calories, 17.6g fat, 4.8g saturated fat, 0.21g sodium

Italian-style roast chicken
A delicious way to roast a chicken as the broth mixes with the meat juices while cooking, making a sauce inside the bird. Serve with all the trimmings and invite your friends over for a feast! **Serves 4–6**

1 large chicken (corn-fed is best)
4 low-salt stock cubes (chicken or vegetable)
4–6 garlic cloves, halved but unpeeled
2 lemons, quartered
2 sprigs of fresh rosemary

Preheat the oven to 425°F.
Place the chicken in your sink and rinse through the cavity to clean.
Break each of the stock cubes into 2–4 pieces. Place a few pieces in the cavity of the chicken, followed by a few halves of garlic, then a quarter of a lemon, squeezing it as you push it in. Repeat until all of the cubes, garlic, and lemon pieces are inside the chicken. Now slide in the rosemary.
Place in a roasting pan and cook in the oven for 1½ hours.

Per serving: 466 calories, 28.7g fat, 8.2g saturated fat, 0.81g sodium

Chinese wok-fried pork

Pork can be a very low-fat lean meat. Just make sure that you buy the right cuts. Ask at the meat counter or butcher if you are unsure. This dish can also be made with chicken. **Serves 4**

2 tablespoons vegetable (canola) oil
2½ lbs lean ground pork
5 oz can water chestnuts, drained
1 garlic clove, crushed
12 button mushrooms, cut in half
4 small bok choy, roughly chopped
4 tablespoons water
1 tablespoon oyster sauce
1 tablespoon reduced-salt soy sauce
4 scallions, chopped
1 inch cube fresh ginger root, finely sliced

Heat the oil in a wok, add the pork and cook for 2–3 minutes, stirring continuously.

Chop the water chestnuts roughly and add to the pan with the garlic, mushrooms, and bok choy.

Add the water and then all the remaining ingredients. Cook for 8 minutes.

Serve with rice.

Per serving: 465 calories, 19.6g fat, 5.5g saturated fat, 0.61g sodium

Saffron chicken

Saffron gives food a delicate flavor and incredible color—a little goes a long way. Serve with Low-fat Chunky French fries or Roast Potatoes with Sage (see page 76) and some greens. **Serves 4**

1 large chicken (corn-fed is best)
1 low-salt stock cube
2 lemons
1 onion, quartered
4–6 garlic cloves, halved
3 sprigs of fresh thyme
3 sprigs of fresh rosemary
1 teaspoon saffron
4 potatoes
1 tablespoon olive oil
1 teaspoon paprika
Freshly ground black pepper

Preheat the oven to 425°F.

Put the chicken in your sink and rinse through the cavity to clean.

Cut both the stock cube and 1 of the lemons into quarters. Now put them, together with the onion and halved garlic cloves, inside the chicken cavity.

Wedge the thyme and rosemary under the skin above the breast and sprinkle the saffron over the chicken.

Trim the ends of the second lemon and cut it into slices 1 inch thick. Put these on top of the chicken and in between the legs. This keeps the chicken moist and helps to dissolve the saffron.

Cook in the oven for 1½ hours.

Meanwhile, peel and quarter the potatoes and boil in water for 8 minutes. Drain the potatoes and put on a baking sheet, adding the oil, paprika, and black pepper. Mix well and roast with the chicken for 40–50 minutes, turning once halfway through the cooking time.

Per serving: 602 calories, 31.4g fat, 0.4g saturated fat, 0.31g sodium

Moroccan lamb on couscous

Make sure you use a lean shoulder of lamb for a wonderful flavor and tender meat. If asparagus isn't in season you could serve with roasted vegetables instead. **Serves 4**

4 large boneless lamb steaks
9 oz uncooked couscous
Juice of 1 lemon
4 scallions, finely chopped
1 tablespoon olive oil
10 large asparagus spears, cut
   into 1 inch pieces
1 garlic clove, crushed

For the marinade
1 tablespoon reduced-salt
   soy sauce
1 teaspoon honey
Drop of olive oil
1 garlic clove, crushed
4 sprigs of fresh rosemary,
   finely chopped
Juice of 1 lemon

Combine all the marinade ingredients together in a large bowl and add to the lamb steaks. Refrigerate for at least an hour so that the flavors are absorbed.

Put the couscous in a bowl and add boiling water to just above the level of the couscous. Cover with a plate to keep in the heat and set aside for 5 minutes. Squeeze over the lemon juice and add the scallions.

In a large wok, heat the olive oil and fry the asparagus. Add the garlic and fry for 2–3 minutes. Add to the couscous and stir well.

Sear the lamb on a high heat in a skillet with a drizzle of olive oil. (I do this for 2–3 minutes on each side as I like it rare; for well done cook for 4 minutes on each side.)

To serve, remove the lamb from the pan, slice each steak into 3 pieces and put on a bed of couscous.

Per serving: 437 calories, 17.1g fat, 6.6g saturated fat, 0.27g sodium

Calf's liver wasabi mash

A classic dish that is always a favorite. The key is to never overcook the liver—fry in a skillet to lock in the juices and keep it tender on the inside. Serve with some English mustard. **Serves 4**

4 large potatoes, quartered
2 teaspoons wasabi paste
4 tablespoons 2% milk
3 tablespoons vegetable
   (canola) oil, plus a little
   more for frying the liver

Freshly ground black pepper
2 medium onions, thinly sliced
4 medium slices calf's liver

Place the potatoes in a saucepan of boiling water and simmer for 20–25 minutes. Drain and mash them with a potato masher or a fork. Mix the wasabi paste with 1 tablespoon of the milk and add to the potatoes. Gradually add the remaining milk and 1 tablespoon of the oil and mash until smooth.
Season with black pepper and set aside.
Next, heat the remaining oil in a large skillet. Add the onions and cook for 3–4 minutes. Turn the heat down and cook for a further 3 minutes on a low heat or until the onions are caramelized. Set aside.
Add a drizzle of oil to a skillet and sear the liver for 2 minutes on each side so that it's nice and pink. (I would even try it for just 1 minute each side to be rare.)
Serve the liver with the mash and top with the onions.

Per serving: 389 calories, 15.3g fat, 2.4g saturated fat, 0.11g sodium

5

Desserts

Chilled strawberry soup with fresh mint

An unusual-sounding dish, perhaps, but strawberry soup is a popular recipe with variations all over the world. Try it—it's a wonderful, fresh dessert. **Serves 4–6**

2 cups red wine

¾ cup brown sugar

2¼ lbs fresh strawberries, hulled

4 tablespoons plain low-fat yogurt

Fresh mint leaves, to garnish

Heat the wine together with the sugar in a large saucepan on a medium heat for 30 minutes until it has reduced and become more of a syrup.

Add the strawberries and cook for a further 2 minutes (or 4 minutes if they are unripe).

Now either refrigerate for serving chilled or serve at room temperature, as you prefer.

Pour some soup and berries into bowls and top with yogurt and mint leaves.

Per serving: 287 calories, 0.4g fat, 0.1g saturated fat, 0.04g sodium

Apricot and orange fool

A perfectly light dessert that is unbelievably easy to make. For those of you who find it hard to make desserts, try this: it's foolproof! Other fruits can be used if you prefer—the choice is yours. **Serves 4**

1 tablespoon almonds

1 cup dried apricots

1 tablespoon honey

2 oranges, peeled

2 oz plain low-fat yogurt

1 tablespoon brown sugar

Toast the almonds in a dry skillet until golden (keep a close eye on them as you don't want them to burn). Set aside.

Put all the ingredients except the almonds in a food-processor and whizz until smooth. Transfer to serving bowls and chill in the fridge until needed.

Top with the toasted almonds to serve.

Per serving: 151 calories, 2.2g fat, 0.4g saturated fat, 0.04g sodium

Poached pears with vanilla

Very easy to make and also works really well if you need to prepare ahead of time. The empty vanilla pod can be put into a canister of sugar to make vanilla sugar. **Serves 4**

8 small pears
Juice of 1 lemon
4 tablespoons brown sugar
½ cup water
3 cups white dessert wine
½ vanilla pod, seeds removed

Peel the pears, keeping the stem on them. As soon as you have done this pour the lemon juice all over the pears to prevent them from turning brown.

Put the pears upright in a large saucepan—you may need to cut the bottoms so that they sit straight.

Add the sugar, water, and wine and simmer on a low heat for 10 minutes, then remove the pears from the pan with a slotted spoon. Put them in either one large dish or individual serving dishes.

Add the vanilla seeds to the remaining liquid and stir over the low heat until it is reduced and syrupy. This will take just a few minutes.

Pour the liquid over the pears and serve.

Per serving: 226 calories, 0.2g fat, 0g saturated fat, 0.03g sodium

Grilled fruit

The fruits used in this recipe are very sweet, so only a little brown sugar is needed to caramelize them under the broiler. Serve with some plain fromage frais or low-fat yogurt. **Serves 6**

2 containers strawberries
1 container blueberries
1 pineapple
2 mangoes
4 tablespoons brown sugar (or 6 if the fruit is on the tart side)
1 teaspoon ground cinnamon

Hull the strawberries, slice in half and put in a large bowl. Add the blueberries.

Remove the skin from the pineapple and take out the core. Slice the flesh into 1 inch wedges and add to the mixing bowl. Peel the mango and slice into 1 inch pieces and add to the bowl.

Now add half the sugar and the cinnamon and mix in really well. Transfer to a baking sheet and sprinkle the remaining sugar on top.

Put under the broiler for 3–5 minutes or until caramelized. Serve warm.

Per serving: 182 calories, 0.6g fat, 0g saturated fat, 0.01g sodium

Caramelized oranges
A wonderful Italian-style dish, this is a handy recipe for when you have lots of oranges that need eating up. Cooked in this way, they will keep for a few weeks in the fridge. **Serves 4**

8 navel oranges
2 large lemons
1¼ cups water
½ cup sugar
⅔ cup dry white wine, plus an extra 2½ tablespoons
2½ tablespoons Grand Marnier

Remove the colored part of orange and lemon rind with a vegetable peeler, cutting from top to bottom to obtain about ½ x 3 inch strips. Slice lengthways into very thin juliennes. Set the lemons aside, then trim the tops and bottoms from the oranges, cutting away any pith. You can either keep the oranges whole or slice them. Set aside in a large serving dish.

Bring the water to a boil in a medium saucepan and add the julienned rind, boiling for 5 minutes. Drain in a colander, then transfer to heavy saucepan.

Add the sugar and the ⅔ cup of wine. Cook on a medium-low heat until the sugar dissolves, then increase the heat to high and boil until the syrup turns a medium caramel color. Remove from the heat and stir in the liqueur with the 2½ tablespoons of wine.

Pour the syrup over the oranges and serve at room temperature.

Per serving: 232 calories, 0.3g fat, 0g saturated fat, 0.02g sodium

Sesame bananas
An easy and healthy alternative to Chinese toffee bananas, and you don't need many ingredients. This is a really comforting dessert that is popular with children and grown-ups alike! **Serves 4–6**

4 bananas
Juice of 1 lemon
4 tablespoons water
½ vanilla pod, seeds removed
½ cup brown sugar
2–3 tablespoons sesame seeds, toasted in a dry skillet

Cut the bananas into 1 inch slices, put in a bowl and squeeze over the lemon juice (this will help the bananas to keep their color). Set aside.

In a saucepan, bring the water, vanilla seeds, and sugar to a boil. Let it boil until it reduces to a thick liquid.

Now quickly (so that it doesn't harden) drizzle the mixture all over the banana pieces.

Sprinkle over the sesame seeds and serve.

Per serving: 246 calories, 3.8g fat, 0.6g saturated fat, 0.01g sodium

Summer puddings
A fat-free version of a classic English summer dish that is full of flavor. I like to do the puddings in individual molds as below, but you could use one big mold if you prefer. **Serves 4**

1 container each strawberries, blueberries, and black currants
14 oz mixed frozen berries, defrosted
½ cup confectioner's sugar, plus extra for dusting
6 slices white bread, crusts removed
Handful of fresh mint leaves

Hull the strawberries, cut each into 4 and add to three-quarters of the mixed frozen fruit. Add half of the sugar and set aside.

Put the rest of the frozen fruit in a blender together with the remaining sugar and whizz to a purée.

Line 4 ramekins or small pudding molds with plastic wrap. Now cut small circles of bread to form the pudding bases, slices for the sides, and larger circles for the tops. Dip the pieces of bread in the purée and use to line the molds.

Fill the centers with the strawberry and frozen fruit mixture and a little of the purée and press down well, topping with the larger circles of bread.

Place the puddings the fridge to chill for 30 minutes.

Remove the puddings from the molds and put on to plates. Pour over the remaining purée and serve, garnished with the blueberries, black currants, and remaining strawberries, a dusting of confectioner's sugar and fresh mint leaves.

Per serving: 216 calories, 1.2g fat, 0.2g saturated fat, 0.23g sodium

Light crème brûlée
This is a healthy and easy way to make crème brûlée. The traditional method is far more complicated, yet you can still achieve all the flavor this way, without it being too rich. **Serves 4**

14 oz raspberries (strawberries can also be used)
1 teaspoon vanilla essence
11 oz plain low-fat yogurt
6 tablespoons Greek yogurt
6 tablespoons brown sugar
4 sprigs of fresh mint

Preheat the broiler to high.

Divide the fruit between 4 ramekins.

Mix together the vanilla essence and yogurt and pour on top of the fruit in each ramekin.

Now add a thin layer of Greek yogurt to each ramekin to prevent the mixture from curdling.

Sprinkle 1½ tablespoons of brown sugar on each ramekin to cover the surface.

Place under the broiler for 2–3 minutes until the sugar has caramelised.

Top with a little fresh mint and serve.

Per serving: 179 calories, 3.1g fat, 1.8g saturated fat, 0.08g sodium

Crêpes with subtropical fruits *A classic French crêpe batter, sweetened with the natural flavors of subtropical fruits. These fruits are readily available; make sure they are nice and ripe.* **Serves 6–8**

1 cup all-purpose flour
1¼ cups 2% milk
3 large eggs
2 tablespoons brown sugar
Cooking spray or a drizzle of
   vegetable (canola) oil

To serve
4 tablespoons maple syrup
4 lemons, quartered
1 ripe mango, peeled and diced
6 lychees, peeled and diced
1 ripe papaya, peeled and
   diced
4 passion fruits

Sift the flour into a bowl and make a well in the middle.
Add the milk and eggs and beat until smooth, then add the sugar and beat again.
Heat a non-stick skillet (preferably a crêpe pan), using a spray oil if you have one, or a drizzle of vegetable oil if not. Reduce to a medium heat and drop a ladleful of the batter on to the pan. Wait for bubbles to appear (1–2 minutes), then flip. Make more crêpes in the same way until you have used up all the batter.
Drizzle each crêpe with maple syrup and a squeeze of lemon, then add a mix of fruit and roll up. Spoon over some passion fruit seeds and serve.

Per serving: 242 calories, 4.8g fat, 1.4g saturated fat, 0.07g sodium

Pumpkin cheesecake
This is a recipe that is a favorite of mine after working in the States. It's easy to make and the cinnamon and pumpkin combination is a marriage made in heaven. A great autumn dessert. **Serves 16**

For the base
6 oz gingersnap crumbs
3 tablespoons brown sugar
2 tablespoons butter, melted

For the filling
3½ cups low-fat cream cheese
¾ cup brown sugar
2 teaspoons ground cinnamon
¼ teaspoon ground nutmeg
¼ teaspoon salt

9 oz canned pumpkin (not fresh)
2 eggs and 2 egg whites
2 tablespoons cornstarch
2 teaspoons vanilla essence

For the topping
1 cup low-fat crème fraîche
1 tablespoon brown sugar
½ teaspoon vanilla essence

Preheat the oven to 400°F.

To make the base, mix the gingersnap crumbs, sugar, and melted butter and press into the bottom of a 9 inch springform cake pan. Bake in the oven for 8 minutes, then set aside on a wire rack to cool.

To make the filling, beat the cream cheese, sugar, cinnamon, nutmeg, and salt until well blended.

Mix in the pumpkin until combined, then beat in the eggs and egg whites until well blended.

Mix in the cornstarch and vanilla essence until blended.

Spoon the cheesecake mixture over the biscuit base and bake for 40–45 minutes or until the center is almost set. Remove from the oven and cool on a wire rack for 5 minutes.

Meanwhile, to make the topping, combine the crème fraîche, sugar, and vanilla and gently spread over the top of the cheesecake. Return to the oven and bake for a further 3–4 minutes until the topping is set.

Remove the cheesecake from the oven and set aside on a wire rack to cool completely. Refrigerate for at least 4 hours before serving.

Per serving: 213 calories, 8.1g fat, 4.2g saturated fat, 0.29g sodium

Raspberry creams
An extremely simple dessert, perfect for a summer's day. These raspberry creams are also a great option if you're looking for a dessert that can be prepared in advance. **Serves 4**

1½ cups fresh raspberries
5 oz low-fat cottage cheese
5 oz plain low-fat yogurt

3 tablespoons sugar
½ teaspoon vanilla essence
4 sprigs of fresh mint

Put all the ingredients (except for the mint) in a blender and whizz until smooth.

Transfer to ramekins and cover with plastic wrap. Refrigerate for at least an hour.

Serve garnished with fresh mint leaves.

Per serving: 115 calories, 0.9g fat, 0.2g saturated fat, 0.14g sodium

Frozen yogurt

I've used raspberries here but any soft fruit will do, and apples and pears work too. If you don't have an ice cream maker, just put the mixture straight in the freezer. It will have a few crystals in it but will taste just as good. **Serves 8**

¾ cup fresh raspberries
1 cup granulated sugar

1¼ lbs plain low-fat yogurt

Put the raspberries in a food-processor and whizz to a smooth purée (around 1 minute). Add the sugar and whizz for a further 30 seconds.

Put the raspberry mixture in a medium-size mixing bowl and fold in the yogurt.

Transfer to an ice cream maker and freeze according to the manufacturer's instructions.

If made in advance, place in the fridge for 30 minutes before serving.

Per serving: 143 calories, 0.8g fat, 0.5g saturated fat, 0.06g sodium

Berry sorbet

Serve this in Martini glasses, garnished with a sprig of mint, either as a course between meals or as a dessert. You can use a mix of berries or just one kind—the choice is yours. **Serves 6**

18 oz fresh berries
Juice and shredded rind of
   1 large orange
2–3 tablespoons orange
   liqueur (such as Cointreau or
   Grand Marnier)

6 fl oz water
2 egg whites
½ cup superfine sugar

Put the fruit, orange juice and rind, liqueur, and water in a food-processor and whizz until smooth. I like to leave the seeds in but you can strain your mixture if you prefer.

If you have an ice-cream maker, churn the mixture until it starts to freeze. Alternatively pour the mixture into a rigid container and freeze, stirring every 30 minutes or so until ice crystals start to form and it feels slushy.

Whisk the egg whites until stiff peaks form, then gradually add the sugar, beating until firm and glossy. Fold the meringue mixture into the fruit mixture and continue to freeze and stir until completely frozen. If made in advance, transfer the mixture to the fridge 30 minutes before serving.

Per serving: 110 calories, 0.3g fat, 0g saturated fat, 0.02g sodium

Light chocolate torte
Normally this delicious dessert is made with double cream and lots of butter, but I'm sure you won't feel that any of the flavor or texture has been compromised in this recipe. **Serves 14**

Cooking spray or vegetable (canola) oil
5 cups all-purpose flour
4 oz unsweetened cocoa powder
2⅓ cups superfine sugar
2 teaspoons bicarbonate baking soda
1 teaspoon baking powder
¼ teaspoon salt
½ teaspoon ground cinnamon
10 oz pitted prunes, puréed
2 teaspoons vanilla essence
2 eggs
1 cup 1% milk
1 cup strong coffee
Confectioner's sugar, for dusting
Handful strawberries, to serve (optional)

Preheat the oven to 350°F and spray or grease a 9 inch cake pan with oil.

In a large mixing bowl, sift together the flour, cocoa, superfine sugar, baking soda, baking powder, salt, and cinnamon.

Add the prunes, vanilla, eggs, and milk and mix well until blended.

Stir the coffee into the mixture, then pour into the prepared cake pan. Bake for 40–45 minutes or until the tip of a knife inserted gently into the center of the cake comes out clean.

Leave to cool for a few minutes, then sift confectioner's sugar over the top of the torte and serve, with strawberries on the side if liked.

Per serving: 204 calories, 4.1g fat, 1.4g saturated fat, 0.31g sodium

Chocolate fridge cake
Chocolate usually takes a while to cook but this recipe is easy, involves no cooking and is not an exact science like most baking. If you add more or less chocolate it will still work! **Serves 6**

4 oz dark chocolate, 70% cocoa solids, broken into pieces
1 tablespoon golden syrup
4 oz low-fat spread
4 oz graham crackers, roughly crushed
3½ oz glacé cherries

Line a 1 lb loaf pan with plastic wrap, leaving a little extra over the edge.

Melt the chocolate, syrup, and butter in a heatproof bowl over a saucepan of gently simmering water. Stir well, then add the crackers and cherries.

Pour into the prepared pan. Fold over the plastic wrap and put it in the fridge to set—this will take 1–2 hours.

To serve, remove the cake from the pan and slice.

Per serving: 339 calories, 20.6g fat, 7.7g saturated fat, 0.27g sodium

Basic Recipes

6

Classic French dressing

This is an essential dressing that just needs nothing more. It tastes great with French bread as a dip or with any salad. Experiment until you find your favorite extra virgin olive oil. **Serves 4–6**

3½ tablespoons extra virgin olive oil
1½ tablespoons white wine vinegar
Juice of 1 lemon
Handful of chopped fresh tarragon leaves
Freshly ground black pepper
Pinch of dried herbes de Provence
2 tablespoons Dijon mustard

Mix all the ingredients together and whisk well until an almost mayonnaise-like consistency is achieved.

Per serving: 116 calories, 12g fat, 1.6g saturated fat, 0.22g sodium

Japanese wasabi dressing

This is a wonderful alternative to an oil-based dressing and is delicious with steamed green vegetables. It's fresh and has a real kick to it. Add as much wasabi as you can handle! **Serves 4–6**

Juice of 1 lemon
1 teaspoon wasabi paste
7 oz low-fat fromage frais or plain low-fat yogurt
Freshly ground black pepper

Mix the lemon juice and wasabi paste together until they are well blended. Add the fromage frais or yogurt and season with black pepper.

Per serving: 29 calories, 0.1g fat, 0g saturated fat, 0.03g sodium

Oriental dressing

This dressing is similar to that used in the Japanese steak houses, and is suitable for drizzling over grilled meat as well as salads. Sesame oil is used here that, like olive oil, is low in saturated fat. **Serves 4–6**

3½ tablespoons vegetable (canola) oil
3½ tablespoons sesame oil
Juice of 4 lemons
2 tablespoons reduced-salt soy sauce
2 tablespoons sesame seeds, toasted in a dry skillet
1 tablespoon wasabi paste
1 inch cube fresh ginger root, shredded

Mix all the ingredients together well.
Using just a few tablespoons of the dressing per salad serving (a little goes a long way), add to your salad in a mixing bowl and mix well. This is better than pouring the dressing over the leaves on individual serving plates.

Per serving: 257 calories, 26.5g fat, 2.9g saturated fat, 0.56g sodium

Tofu guacamole
This is my take on the classic avocado dip, with tofu added to lighten it. It is an easy way to get more of the super-healthy soya protein into your diet, that is known for its cholesterol-lowering benefits. **Serves 4–6**

3 ripe avocados
Juice of 1 lime
Handful of fresh cilantro, chopped

8 oz tofu
1 small red bird's eye chile
4 scallions, chopped

Put all the ingredients except the scallions into a food-processor and blend to a chunky dip (not a purée).
Add the scallions and mix in well.
Serve with warm pita bread, crudités, or bread sticks.

Per serving: 221 calories, 20.7g fat, 2.5g saturated fat, 0.01g sodium

Salsa
Salsas are used as dips but they can also work as an alternative to salad dressing, as well as making a superb partner for egg dishes such as omelets. Spice this recipe up as much as you want by adding more chile. **Serves 4**

8 large plum tomatoes, halved
Freshly ground black pepper
1 red onion, finely chopped
4 scallions, finely sliced

1 small red bird's eye chile
Juice of 1 lime
Handful of fresh cilantro, roughly chopped
1 garlic clove, crushed

Scoop the seeds out of the tomatoes, but do not worry if a few remain. Dice the tomato flesh, put in a bowl, and season with black pepper.
Add the red onion to the tomatoes, followed by the scallions. Mix well.
Chop the chile as finely as possible and add to the mixture, along with the lime juice, cilantro, and garlic.

Per serving: 55 calories, 0.8g fat, 0.1g saturated fat, 0.02g sodium

Thai dipping sauce
This Thai dipping sauce is easy to make and doesn't have any of the preservatives and artificial flavorings found in so many bottled sauces. And, most important, it tastes a million times better. **Serves 2–4**

2 tablespoons superfine sugar
Juice of 1 lime
6 tablespoons water

2 tablespoons white wine vinegar
3 red bird's eye chiles, thinly sliced (use the seeds)

Put all the ingredients in a saucepan and bring to a boil. Cook for 1 minute, then serve with fishcakes, chicken, duck, or meat.

Per serving: 63 calories, 0g fat, 0g saturated fat, 0g sodium

Low-fat hummous
If you're looking for a lower-fat hummous, try this recipe. It tastes great, even without the tahini. Serve as a dip with warm pita bread and crudités or just spread it on toast as a snack. **Serves 4**

16 oz can garbanzo beans
1 garlic clove
3 tablespoons plain low-fat yogurt or fromage frais

Juice of 1 lemon
Freshly ground black pepper
Drizzle of extra virgin olive oil (optional)

Empty the beans into a strainer and rinse through, then drain.
Put all the ingredients, except for the olive oil, in a blender and mix to a smooth paste.
Add a little oil on top of the finished dish to taste if desired.

Per serving: 86 calories, 2.1g fat, 0.1g saturated fat, 0.16g sodium

Tzatziki
A classic Greek dip. Usually this has raw garlic in it, but my version uses roasted garlic, making it less pungent. This is ideal for dipping raw vegetables such as carrots, cucumber, and peppers into. **Serves 4–6**

1 garlic bulb
Extra virgin olive oil
1 medium cucumber
7 oz plain low-fat yogurt

Handful of fresh mint, shredded
7 oz low-fat fromage frais
Juice of 1 large lemon

Preheat the oven to 350°F.
Slice through the middle of the garlic bulb and drizzle with olive oil. Push the two halves back together and wrap in aluminum foil. Put in the oven and cook for 30 minutes.
Meanwhile, slice the cucumber in half lengthways, scoop out the seeds, and discard. Cut the cucumber into thin strips and put in a mixing bowl.
In a separate bowl, put the yogurt, mint, fromage frais, and lemon juice and mix together well.
Remove the garlic from the oven and mix 4 cloves into the yogurt mixture. (The rest of the garlic can be kept in the fridge, wrapped in aluminum foil.) Add to the cucumber and mix well.
Serve with crudités or pita bread.

Per serving: 69 calories, 1.4g fat, 0.5g saturated fat, 0.06g sodium

Eggplant dip

This is perfect to serve with crudités or pita bread. Normally eggplant is cooked with lots of oil as it absorbs it all, but this is a great way to cook it without all that fat. **Serves 6 as an appetizer**

1 large eggplant
2 tablespoons olive oil, plus a little extra for brushing
Freshly ground black pepper
2 garlic cloves
3 tablespoons balsamic vinegar
Handful of fresh parsley, finely chopped

Preheat the oven to 375°F.

Cut the eggplant in half lengthways, brush with olive oil and season with black pepper. Put in the oven and cook for 35 minutes.

Remove the eggplant from the oven and, using a spoon, scoop out all the flesh. Put in a blender with the olive oil, garlic, and vinegar and whizz to a chunky texture.

Stir in the parsley and serve.

Per serving: 54 calories, 4.5g fat, 0.6g saturated fat, 0g sodium

Tomato and feta dip

This is an easy dish to make and great to serve for friends with plenty of crusty French bread for mopping. I also use the leftovers as a pasta sauce—in fact it's a good idea to make extra for this reason! **Serves 4–6**

5 tablespoons olive oil or vegetable (canola) oil
$1\frac{1}{4}$ lbs cherry tomatoes
1 garlic clove, crushed
$1\frac{1}{3}$ cups feta cheese
Freshly ground black pepper
Large handful of fresh basil leaves

Put the oil and cherry tomatoes in a large skillet and heat on a medium heat.

After a few minutes add the garlic to the pan.

Cut the feta cheese into ¼ inch cubes and add to the pan.

Season with pepper (not salt as the feta cheese has a salty taste). Continue to heat until it all just starts to blend and the cheese begins to melt.

Remove from the heat and transfer to a large serving bowl.

Slice the basil and add to the dish before serving.

Per serving: 278 calories, 24.5g fat, 8.2g saturated fat, 0.74g sodium

Olive tapenade

There are so many ways to use this —on top of fish before you cook it, on top of bread, or served as a dip with crudités. It will keep well in the fridge for a few weeks.

Serves 4–6

1 tablespoon Dijon mustard
Handful of fresh basil leaves
1 garlic clove
Juice of ½ lemon
1 tablespoon capers

2 tablespoons extra virgin
    olive oil
15 oz can pitted black olives,
    drained

Put all the ingredients in a food-processor and whizz to a chunky mix.

Per serving: 154 calories, 16.4g fat, 2g saturated fat, 0.57g sodium

Vegetable broth

Making your own broth need not be a chore. This is a simple way to make it and you'll see for yourself the difference in the taste alone. Fresh is always best.

Makes 2½ cups

2 carrots, chopped
2 onions, quartered
2 celery sticks, roughly
    chopped
½ fennel bulb, roughly
    chopped
Stalk from a head of broccoli,
    roughly chopped

4 large tomatoes
8 button mushrooms, halved
6 black peppercorns
1 dried bay leaf
4 tablespoons tomato paste
3 fresh parsley stalks

Place all the ingredients in a large saucepan, cover with water, and simmer for 50 minutes.
Strain and use the broth for soups, risottos, and more. You can purée the remaining ingredients (minus the bay leaf) for an alternative soup.

Per 100ml: 18 calories, 0.1g fat, 0g saturated fat, 0.05g sodium

Fish broth

This broth is not hard to make. Always use celery, carrot, and onions as staples and you will not go wrong, then you can try being creative by adding your own choice of herbs and spices. **Makes 2½ cups**

6 large tiger shrimp
Heads, skin, and bones of 4 fish
  (sea bass, salmon, trout, or
  any fish of that size will do)
OR
4 whole trout, cut into
  4 pieces each (a more
  economical option)

2 carrots, chopped
2 onions, quartered
2 celery sticks, roughly
  chopped
3 garlic cloves, halved
4 large tomatoes
4 tablespoons tomato paste
3 fresh parsley stalks

Put all the ingredients in a large saucepan, cover with water, and simmer for 50 minutes. Strain and use as required.
You can put the remaining ingredients in a blender with ⅔ cup of the broth to make an instant fish soup.

Per 100ml: 22 calories, 0.2g fat, 0g saturated fat, 0.06g sodium

Chicken broth

The key to a good chicken broth is to refrigerate it, then skim off the fat from the surface. This also makes it much more healthy. Homemade broth can be stored in the fridge for a few days and also freeze well. **Makes 2½ cups**

1 chicken, cut into 8 pieces
6 button mushrooms
Scant teaspoon salt
1 teaspoon black peppercorns
2 carrots, chopped
2 onions, chopped

2 celery sticks, roughly
  chopped
3 garlic cloves, halved
4 large tomatoes
3 fresh parsley stalks

Put all the ingredients in a large saucepan, cover with water and simmer for 50 minutes.
Strain, leave to cool, and then refrigerate. After an hour remove the layer of fat from the top, using a large metal spoon, then reheat the broth and use as required.
Add noodles for a great chicken soup and save the vegetables from the broth to serve with it.

Per 100ml: 17 calories, 0.2g fat, 0g saturated fat, 0.27g sodium

Index

Resources

US

American Heart Association
National Center
7272 Greenville Avenue
Dallas
TX 75231
1-800-AHA-USA-1 (1-800-242-8721)
www.americanheart.org

American Stroke Association
www.strokeassociation.org

American Diabetic Association
www.eatright.org

CANADA

Heart and Stroke Foundation of Canada
1825 Park Road S.E.
Calgary
Alberta T2G 3Y6
(403) 264 5549
www.heartandstroke.ca

UK

British Heart Foundation
14 Fitzhardinge Street
London
W1H 6DH
020 7935 0185
Heart information line:
08450 708 070 (Mon-Fri, 9-5)
www.bhf.org.uk

H·E·A·R·T UK
7 North Road
Maidenhead
Berkshire
SL6 1PE
01628 628 638
www.heartuk.org.uk

British Dietetic Association
Charles House, Great Charles Street
Queensway, Birmingham
West Midlands B3 3HT
0121 200 8080
www.bda.uk.com

AUSTRALIA

National Heart Foundation of Australia
Cnr Denison St & Geils Court
Deakin
ACT 2600
1300 36 27 87
www.heartfoundation.com.au

Heart Support Australia
PO Box 266
Mawson
ACT 2607
0262 852357
www.heartnet.org.au

Published in 2008 by Kyle Books,
an imprint of Kyle Cathie Ltd
www.kylecathie.com

Distributed by National Book Network
4501 Forbes Blvd., Suite 200
Lanham, MD 20706
Phone: (301) 459 3366 Fax: (301) 429 5746

Daniel Green and Catherine Collins are hereby identified as the authors of this work in accordance with Section 77 of the Copyright, Designs and Patents Act 1988.

Text © 2007 Daniel Green and Catherine Collins
Photography © 2007 Lis Parsons
Book design © 2007 Kyle Cathie Limited

Project editor Jennifer Wheatley
Designer Carl Hodson
Photographer Lis Parsons
Home economist Lorna Brash
Styling Penny Markham
Copyeditor Anne Newman
Editorial assistant Vicki Murrell
Recipe analysis Dr Wendy Doyle
Production Sha Huxtable and Alice Holloway

Library of Congress Control Number:
2008925803

Color reproduction by Colourscan
Printed and bound in Singapore by Star Standard